Breadfruit Buccaneers and the Bounty Bible

by
DAVID MARSHALL

SPECIAL BICENTENNIAL EDITION

A fresh look at the mutiny on HMS *Bounty* and the story of the Pitcairn Island colony over two centuries.

ISBN 0-904748-49-9

STANBOROUGH PRESS
GRANTHAM ENGLAND

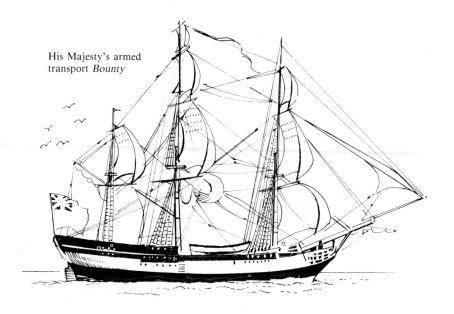

His Majesty's armed transport *Bounty*

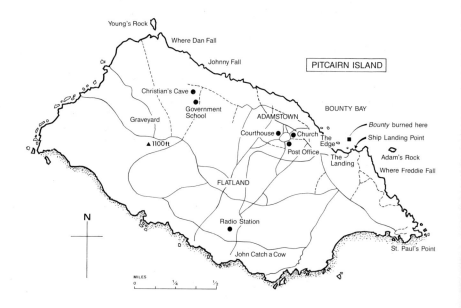

Young's Rock

Where Dan Fall

Johnny Fall

PITCAIRN ISLAND

Christian's Cave

Government School

Graveyard

ADAMSTOWN

BOUNTY BAY

Courthouse

Church

Bounty burned here

The Edge

Ship Landing Point

▲ 1100 ft

Post Office

The Landing

Adam's Rock

Where Freddie Fall

FLATLAND

N

Radio Station

John Catch a Cow

St. Paul's Point

MILES

0   ¼   ½

FOREWORD

by GLYNN CHRISTIAN, BBC TV personality
and descendant of the famous mutineer

For almost two centuries the story of HMS *Bounty* and the fate of the men who took her from her captain has enthralled the world.

Pitcairn and Pitcairn Islanders are today only little removed from the pattern of life established by the mutineers and their Tahitian wives. Food, language, customs and hospitality fuse into a seamless robe of fellowship and interdependent daily life to form something truly unique. Such is the basis for Pitcairn's continuous inspiration of others.

Dr. David Marshall's bright journalistic style makes this new book both a perfect introduction to the most fascinating of sea sagas, and a stimulating refresher course for those who already know the story. A few parts of the story, of course, will never be carved into the stone of verifiable fact. But none of it is fiction.

Pitcairn Island and the Pitcairn Islanders are part of today's world – or should be. Practical assistance to regenerate the island and stimulate population growth is vital. Only constant reminders of the reality of Pitcairn today will attract that sense of responsibility, attract the finance for a vessel and for a stronger infrastructure that sensibly takes the best of twentieth-century technology without sacrificing traditional family and community values. Nothing is more likely to help achieve this than such books as BREADFRUIT, BUCCANEERS AND THE BOUNTY BIBLE. It will help Pitcairn celebrate its Bicentenary in 1990, and ensure that it flourishes on into its third century.

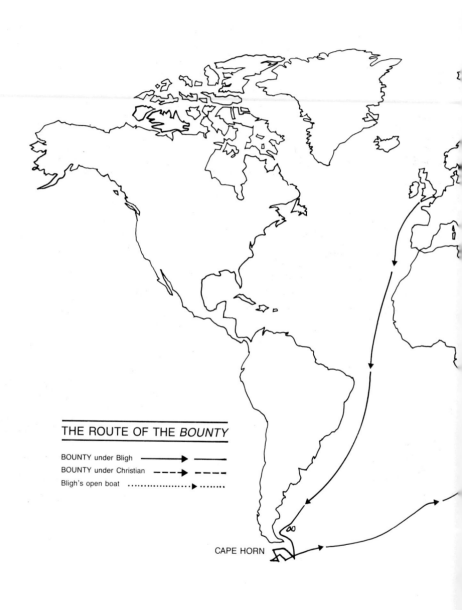

THE ROUTE OF THE *BOUNTY*

BOUNTY under Bligh ⸻▶ ⸻

BOUNTY under Christian ⸺ ▶ ⸺ ⸺

Bligh's open boat ⋯⋯⋯⋯▶ ⋯⋯

CAPE HORN

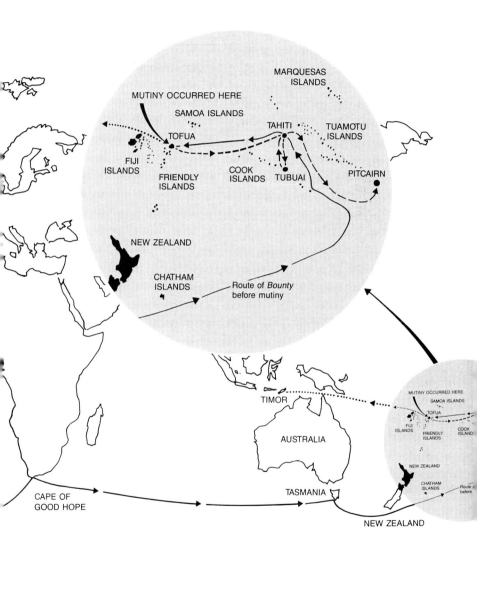

MARQUESAS
ISLANDS

MUTINY OCCURRED HERE

SAMOA ISLANDS

TAHITI

TOFUA

TUAMOTU
ISLANDS

FIJI
ISLANDS

FRIENDLY
ISLANDS

COOK
ISLANDS

TUBUAI

PITCAIRN

NEW ZEALAND

CHATHAM
ISLANDS

Route of *Bounty*
before mutiny

TIMOR

AUSTRALIA

TASMANIA

CAPE OF
GOOD HOPE

NEW ZEALAND

CONTENTS

JOHN ADAMS
The only survivor of the mutineers
who found a new way of life after
reading Fletcher Christian's Bible.

THE MUTINY

THE DARKEST HOUR. 4am and the darkest hour before dawn.

The night had been restless.

The air was clammy, all but unbreathable. It was as if Bligh's 1,015 bread-fruit plants, occupying the great cabin forward of the aft hatchway, were inhaling all available air and exhaling a dampish stench.

Some slept, but fitfully. Others wandered about. There was movement on the forecastle and quarterdeck. A group looked at the volcano erupting on an island not thirty miles away and wondered if it would set the heavens afire. One man saw a water spout 'no great distance from us'. Another was preoccupied with the antics of an abnormally large shark which, in turn, seemed to be preoccupied with the ship.

Fletcher Christian had scarcely scrambled into his bunk behind a canvas screen on the starboard side of HMS *Bounty*'s main hatchway when the ladder thudded to the tread of Midshipman George Stewart. The third watch began at 4, and it was time he was up and active. Although he had not been taken on as a warrant officer, Christian had been assigned this watch, told to assume the duties of a lieutenant and made, in effect, Bligh's second-in-command.

Stewart was especially eager that the master's mate should be seen to be on his watch, and followed Christian to his post.

The events of the previous afternoon had left nerves drawn taut like guitar strings. But, in the nature of things, none would be more likely to snap than Christian's. With a grim concern for both ship and shipmate Stewart held him in determined conversation. He had watched the 24-year-old Christian's preparations for desertion. If he had tried to keep them a secret he had not succeeded; it was rumoured below decks that he was about to jump ship.

During the previous evening Christian had given away the odds and ends he had kept from those months on Tahiti. Had been seen tearing his letters and papers and throwing them overboard. Was known to have applied to the carpenter for nails. Had been heard in earnest barter for items too obviously associated with escape. Was rumoured to have been seen lashing timbers together . . . *to make a raft?*

It would be a suicidal venture, urged Stewart. He should forget it. He would never make it through the shark-infested waters to land. Even if he did reach shore, was *he* not the one who had found out to his cost how inaptly named the Friendly Islands were? He would never escape without a 'Man overboard!' cry. *Then* what would Bligh do? His ill temper was notorious. Until now he had taken it out on his second-in-command; in his absence he would take it out on everyone else.

Stewart had finished his watch. His last, urgent words to Christian as he went below: 'When you go, Christian, the people (the ratings) are ripe for anything.'

INCITEMENT TO MUTINY.   Left alone, Christian reflected that Stewart's last desperate appeal to loyalty could also be interpreted as an incitement to mutiny. The thought flashed across his mind: Why should *he* go? Why not Bligh?

Later Stewart would testify that Christian was 'much out of order' and in 'agony of mind'. Not, however, to the extent that he did not know what he was doing. Instinctively he did the rounds of his duty. Made sure Thomas Ellison with John Mills had assumed the helm. Sent to find out why John Hallet (15) and Thomas Hayward (17) had not reported for duty. Ordered that the decks be swabbed.

Perhaps he would have been trapped by the day's routine, prevented from either desertion or mutiny, had it not been for the fact that others were also 'much out of

10

order' and in 'agony of mind'. Following the mutiny, his brother Edward Christian, a professor of law, found evidence that *each man* was at breaking point . . . .

Midshipman Edward Young's move may have decided Christian. Young's instincts dictated fight, not flight. At 22 he was reckless in his desperation. His motives for approaching the *Bounty*'s second-in-command were very different from Stewart's, though at first his advice may have sounded similar. It would be death to desert. The ratings were ripe for rebellion. Let him at least find out where the men stood. It was still dark. Bligh, Fryer (the master), Cole (the bo'sun), along with Peckover and Elphinstone (whom Christian had leapfrogged in the promotion stakes) were sound asleep. They needed control of the arms chests, but there need be no bloodshed. Bligh and his supporters could be set afloat in the cutter.

Fed on these ideas, Christian's mind began to race, his plans to solidify. When Young left him – going below to await events – he left him fighting with thoughts of the price of mutiny. But was that price any higher than the price of desertion?

4.30am. Still dark except for the unnatural fire of the volcano.

5am. Only the faintest glimmer of dawn astern. And Christian began to incite a mutiny.

He approached Matthew Quintal, muscular, wild, 21. Then Isaac Martin, lean, morose, 30 and, at 5 foot 9 inches, almost as tall as Christian himself. Both men had been flogged. Both believed they had been victimized. Christian told them he intended to take the ship – 'but there is to be no murder'. Both wanted in.

Throwing caution to the winds they began to advise Christian on the disposition of their shipmates.

Charles Churchill. A hard case if ever there was one. He had already deserted once, been put in irons, and flogged at least twice. John Adams (at this time going under the name of Alexander Smith), Bill McKoy, Matt Thompson, Jack Williams: all had strong reasons for hating Bligh.

Christian knew that these, even assuming they could be counted on, would be insufficient out of a ship's company of forty-six. Control of the arms chests would be decisive if he were to receive the support of others. The extent of Christian's anger and desperation showed through here more than at any other time. The success of the mutiny was far from inevitable. He took the conscious decision to fight even if he could only count on the support of a handful of roughnecks.

MUTINY!   Quintal, McKoy and Christian went below to rouse Joseph Coleman, the armourer. His support for the mutiny was decisive. With his keys they went to the two arms chests, on each of which they found the missing midshipmen of Christian's watch, Hallet and Tom Hayward. Christian barked them awake and to their duty.

The arms were distributed. Christian himself took a musket, a fixed bayonet, a pistol, a box of cartridges – and a cutlass!

5.30am, with the sun rising from the sea, the mutiny was well under way. On deck, abaft the mizzen mast, Christian mustered the crew in silence. Quintal, Martin, Churchill, McKoy, Burkett and Lamb were armed.

Quintal had been below rousing the ratings.

Three more men joined the mutineers from the hatchway: John Sumner, John Adams, and Henry Hillbrant. They were soon given arms.

Ellison and Mills quit the helm and joined Christian's group. The two tardy youths – Hallet and Hayward – proved surly. Martin was ordered to guard them.

Christian could now control the upper deck. The three or four others on deck who had not actually joined the mutiny were cowed.

Below, in their cabins, the captain and the master were still asleep. Bligh's cabin was on the starboard side and Fryer's on the port side of the ship.

BLIGH'S DOWNFALL.   Now was the time to take Captain Bligh.

Christian, with Churchill, Mills, Adams, and Burkett went below. They burst into the 6 by 7 foot cabin. It was a rude awakening for Bligh to find five armed men squeezed into his tiny quarters while he lay vulnerable on his bunk.

'Just before sunrising, while I was yet asleep,' the captain wrote some months later, 'Mr. Christian, with the master-at-arms, gunner's mate and Thomas Burkett, seaman, came into my cabin and, seizing me, tied my hands with a cord behind my back, threatening me with instant death if I spoke or made the least noise. I, however, called as loud as I could, in hopes of assistance; but they had already secured the officers who were not of their party by placing sentinels at their doors.'

There was hardly a man aboard who did not hear Bligh roaring 'Murder!' That voice turned up to full volume when the captain was angry or abusive was a familiar sound to the ship's company. But when it registered fear it sent an involuntary shudder through many.

'I was hauled out of my bed and forced on deck in my shirt, suffering great pain from the tightness with which they had tied my hands', wrote Bligh. 'I demanded the reason for such violence, but received no other answer than abuse for not holding my tongue.'

Others said that Bligh was given the reason instantly, that it came from Christian and that it was spat out with great bitterness. 'Can you ask, Captain Bligh, can you ask when you know you have treated us officers and all these poor fellows like Turks?'

With Bligh hollering 'Murder!' the ship was put into a state of confusion. Everyone rushed to the deck as if to abandon ship. As he continued to roar curses and obscentities and was, himself, unceremoniously hauled on deck, those not already aware of what was happening soon found out. Only Muspratt and Millward threw in their lot with the mutineers.

Fryer, the master and no friend of Bligh (or Christian for that matter), awoke to Bligh's roaring. There was an air of unreality as, through the glass panel of his door, he saw the night-shirted Bligh, arms tied behind his back, bundled up the ladder.

Before he could collect his thoughts Quintal broke into his cabin, adrenalin pumping, and announced: 'You are arrested.'

Fryer's standing with the entire crew was low. Christian may well have dismissed him as lazy, less than a man. No one thought he was of the stuff of which heroes were made.

Crisis brought out the best in him.

With iron in his tone the master warned Quintal of the consequences of mutiny; there would be no escape, no hiding place in the oceans of the world from the king's navy. He and his fellows would, without doubt, be found, tried and hanged.

Above the rumble of feet running on the creaking boards, and the shouting coming from the deck, the master demanded to know what was to happen to Bligh. When he was told that the bo'sun was about to hoist the cutter, Fryer exploded: 'The small cutter's bottom is almost out. It is very much eaten with worms. I demand to be allowed on deck to see Captain Bligh.'

Threats to his life from Quintal, then Sumner, both fully armed, failed to silence him. He insisted that his demand to see Bligh be taken to Christian. It was. With reluctance Christian allowed Fryer on deck.

He confronted Bligh as he had never seen him before. Totally bereft of dignity, tied, hands behind, to the mizzen, his night-shirt caught up in the rope exposing his buttocks.

Bligh's version: 'I continued my endeavours to turn the tide of affairs, when Christian changed the cutlass which he had in his hand for a bayonet that was brought to him, holding me with a strong grip by the cord that tied my hands, he, with many oaths, threatened to kill me immediately if I would not be quiet. The villains round me had their pieces cocked and bayonets fixed.'

Fryer was astonished at Bligh's foolhardiness given his desperate situation. He heard him daring his captors to

14

fire on him with their cocked muskets.

In the midst of the chaos that reigned at this stage in the mutiny Fryer repeatedly, and courageously, challenged Christian and the other armed men: 'Mr. Christian, consider what you are about.'

In the confusion it became clear that Christian and his armed supporters intended to put Bligh and those still loyal to him in the cutter. Again Fryer protested the unseaworthiness of the small cutter; its bottom was rotten, the loyal men would stand no chance in shark-infested seas. They should be given a chance in the launch.

When his idea was not immediately taken up Fryer approached Bligh and, *sotto voce*, suggested that, as a last resort, he (Fryer) should remain on board with a view to retaking the ship. After all, the loyalities of a number of the men, including Peckover, an officer, were not yet known. He might be able to swing them over.

Bligh rudely ignored him and shrieked hysterically: 'Knock Christian down.'

No one moved.

In the hope that his words to Bligh had not been overheard, Fryer asked permission to visit Peckover, still confined below with David Nelson the botanist. Incredibly, permission was given. Despite his best efforts, the master failed to stir them into action: they had given up. They looked at Fryer as if he were naïve, attempting a hopeless venture.

When Fryer returned on deck he was ordered back to his cabin.

Bligh's personal servant and cook, John Smith, was ordered below to pick up the captain's clothes. He was also ordered to issue a measure of navy grog to all members of the crew.

Fryer had been successful in one respect. The launch was now hoisted in place of the cutter. This would give Bligh, and any who chose to support him, a chance in the South Seas.

Christian was now in total control. It was evident to him who could and who could not be counted on. Those who had declared themselves for Bligh were ordered into the launch. Finally Bligh himself, now fully dressed, was ordered in with them. Supplies, including a 28-gallon cask of water, 150 pounds of bread, along with a little rum, were also put into the launch. Bligh was allowed a quadrant and a compass. He was given no map, sextant, timekeeper, or any of his surveys and drawings. 'To Mr. Samuel,' wrote Bligh, 'I am indebted for securing my journals and commission, with some material ship's papers. Without these I have nothing to certify what I had done, and my honour and character might have been suspected without my possessing a proper document to have defended them.' Bligh was supplied with four cutlasses and when the carpenter threw in his lot with him he was allowed to take his tool chest.

Twenty-five men remained on board the *Bounty*. Nineteen sailed away in the launch.

Bligh judged (correctly) that at least four of those who remained with Christian were still loyal.

It was 28 April 1789. The *Bounty*'s crew had been together nineteen months. Now Bligh and his nineteen loyal men had 3,600 miles of open ocean to cross in a 23-foot launch: an impossible task.

On HMS *Bounty* the mutineers had begun an adventure that has captured the imagination of the world ever since.

Those who were set adrift in the launch with CAPTAIN BLIGH:

JOHN FRYER *Master*
THOMAS LEDWARD *Acting-Surgeon*
DAVID NELSON *Botanist*
WILLIAM PECKOVER *Gunner*
WILLIAM COLE *Boatswain*
WILLIAM PURCELL *Carpenter*
WILLIAM ELPHINSTONE *Master's Mate*
THOMAS HAYWARD *Midshipman*
JOHN HALLET *Midshipman*
JOHN NORTON *Quartermaster*
PETER LINKLETTER *Quartermaster*
LAWRENCE LeBOGUE *Sailmaker*
JOHN SMITH *Cook*
THOMAS HALL *Cook*
GEORGE SIMPSON *Quartermaster's Mate*
ROBERT TINKLER *A boy*
ROBERT LAMB *Butcher*
Mr. SAMUEL *Clerk*

Those who remained aboard the *Bounty*

FLETCHER CHRISTIAN *Master's Mate*
PETER HEYWOOD *Midshipman*
EDWARD YOUNG *Midshipman*
GEORGE STEWART *Midshipman*
CHARLES CHURCHILL *Master-at-Arms*
JOHN MILLS *Gunner's Mate*
JAMES MORRISON *Boatswain's Mate*
THOMAS BURKETT *Able Seaman*
MATTHEW QUINTAL *Able Seaman*
JOHN SUMNER *Able Seaman*
JOHN MILLWARD *Able Seaman*
WILLIAM McKOY *Able Seaman*
HENRY HILLBRANT *Able Seaman*
MICHAEL BYRNE *Able Seaman**
WILLIAM MUSPRATT *Able Seaman*
ALEXANDER SMITH (John Adams) *Able Seaman*
JOHN WILLIAMS *Able Seaman*
THOMAS ELLISON *Able Seaman*
ISAAC MARTIN *Able Seaman*
RICHARD SKINNER *Able Seaman*
MATTHEW THOMPSON *Able Seaman*
WILLIAM BROWN *Gardener*
JOSEPH COLEMAN *Armourer**
CHARLES NORMAN *Carpenter's Mate**
THOMAS McINTOSH *Carpenter's Crew**

'In all twenty-five hands, and the most able men of the ship's company.'
WILLIAM BLIGH.

* Those detained aboard HMS *Bounty* against their will.

17

A VOYAGE TO TAHITI

BLIGH AND CHRISTIAN.   William Bligh, 34 at the time of the mutiny, was 5 foot 8 inches, the son of a Plymouth customs officer. He went to sea at 16 and soon came to the attention of his superior officers as a lad of exceptional skill in the areas of navigation and map-drawing.

By 1776 Bligh had been noticed by the greatest English explorer of all time, Captain James Cook. In that year Cook took him aboard HMS *Resolution* as master and employed him as a navigator and cartographer. *Discovery* was part of the same venture.

The ship's companies on both *Resolution* and *Discovery* testified to Bligh's tremendous technical skills. But they noted also his uncertain temper, his seeming inability to establish stable friendships, his uncouth ways and language and his extreme vulnerability.

England's national hero James Cook lost his life on this voyage with Bligh. Many on the voyage held Bligh responsible (indirectly) for the great man's death. Cook's relationships with the people of Hawaii had become strained, but an emergency had led him to go ashore at a highly sensitive time. When the crews of *Resolution* and *Discovery* saw Cook and others being marched to the beach by Hawaiian chiefs they opened fire. This precipitate action led the Hawaiians to murder Cook. The first to open fire had been William Bligh. . . .

'Emotional', 'passionate' and 'volatile' are all adjectives used to describe Bligh. They could as easily have been used to describe Fletcher Christian. Ten years Bligh's junior, Christian was 5 feet 10 inches, well built, brown-skinned and dark-haired. Though subject to moods and depression, he was good at human relationships. He was a popular figure and, at his best, amusing and entertaining. An officer who sailed with him in the days before the

18

Bounty expedition wrote: 'He had a blithe, pleasing countenance, and a tall, commanding figure, well adapted to feats of strength and agility.' Ashore, his charm and swashbuckling self-confidence made him the first focus for female attention.

Christian went to Cockermouth Grammar School for seven years. His last year there coincided with the first year of the poet William Wordsworth (Wordsworth later transferred to Hawkshead). The Christian and Wordsworth families had close ties of personal friendship. When Edward Christian tried to clear his brother Fletcher's name following the mutiny he had a staunch ally in William Wordsworth. Nevertheless, there is no evidence of a *personal* friendship at any stage between the great poet and the famous mutineer.

Though from a good family, Christian had no distaste for the tough life at sea with all its privations. He enlisted in the Royal Navy in 1782 when England was at war with France, Spain and the Netherlands *and* was still attempting to crush the revolt among the American colonists.

After only two years at sea he was given a watch aboard HMS *Eurydice*, rare, almost unknown for one so young. It seemed virtually certain that he would become a lieutenant (years before Bligh had attained the same rank). Christian had been to Africa, India and the West Indies. Neither from Captain Courtney of HMS *Eurydice* nor from Captain Bligh on *Britannia* (the first of his voyages with Bligh) was there any suggestion that Christian was in any way a trouble-maker. To the contrary. From both captains he received excellent recommendations.

On his return from his first voyage Fletcher Christian was shattered to discover the news of his mother's bankruptcy. Nevertheless, the Christian family on both the Isle of Man and in Cumbria continued to be treated with great respect and were regarded as being of the highest rank. Fletcher's brother was a professor of law and his uncle the Bishop of Carlisle. But the bankruptcy had a profound personal effect upon Fletcher Christian and, in part at least, accounted for his eagerness to enlist under Bligh and his financial dependence on Bligh which gave the older man an advantage over him and a weapon with which to taunt him.

The circumstances which had brought Bligh and Christian together initially had been Bligh's marriage in 1780 to a lady on the Isle of Man. Bligh wrote of her as being 'well connected'. Among her 'connections' were the influential Heywood and Christian families.

Peter Heywood, 14, owed his position as acting midshipman aboard the *Bounty* to Bligh's Manx connection. And it was the Manx connection that originally recommended Fletcher Christian to Bligh. On their first voyage to the South Seas aboard *Britannia* Bligh had found Christian a first-class navigator, and Christian had benefited much from Bligh's tutelage. That Christian should sail with him yet again, this time aboard *Bounty*, however, was something of a last-minute decision. Bligh replied to Christian's letter of application politely regretting that he had a full complement of officers. Fletcher Christian's swift letter back convinced Bligh that he had the right spirit, and he changed his mind. Christian had offered to do the work of a rating on the condition that he could mess as an officer. He was appointed master's mate.

Bligh's *Narrative* of the *Bounty* expedition was written some months after the event, following his epic 3,900-mile Pacific voyage in the launch. In addition, during Bligh's second bread-fruit voyage, 1791-93, his friends Sir Joseph Banks and James Burney made substantial additions to the narrative, as well as considerable deletions, so that nothing would appear to the advantage of the mutineers in its published form.

Nevertheless, despite Bligh's reinstatement and subsequent success in the Royal Navy, the faults in his character which gave cause for complaint on the *Bounty* remained and continued to be the cause of complaint. Fletcher Christian's equivalent on the 'second bread-fruit voyage', 1791-93, was first lieutenant Francis Bond. The vessel used was the *Providence*. In December 1792 Bond wrote to his brother in England: 'Yes, Tom, our relation

20

(Bligh) had the credit of being a tyrant in his last expedition, where his misfortunes and good fortunes have elevated him to a situation he is incapable of supporting with decent modesty. The very high opinion he has of himself makes him hold everyone of our profession with contempt, perhaps envy. . . . I don't mean to depreciate his extensive knowledge as a seaman and a nautical astronomer, but condemn that want of modesty in self-estimation. To be less prolix I will inform you that he has treated me (nay, all on board) with insolence and arrogance. . . . And notwithstanding his passion is partly to be attributed to a nervous fever, with which he has been attacked most of the voyage, the chief part of his conduct must have arisen from the fury of an ungovernable temper.' Bond's letter goes on to give details. Bligh's intent seems to have been to humiliate the senior officers by forcing them to participate in menial tasks – including swabbing the decks – while supervising the common seamen. Bligh's permission had to be solicited on every point. He would not delegate. There was evidence that he had singled Bond out on many occasions for ridicule in front of the crew. . . .

Similar complaints with regard to Bligh's conduct were made when he was removed as governor of New South Wales, a position which he held from 1806 to 1810. The minutes of the courts martial of Lieutenant Frazier (1805), Short (1807), Kent (1811) and Johnstone (1811) all confirm Bligh's gift for vindictiveness and abusive language. Indeed, Bligh himself was convicted in a court martial for using abusive language to a junior officer and was regarded as one catalyst in the fleet-wide Nore mutiny.

Bligh's third lieutenant on the *Providence* during the second bread-fruit voyage was George Tobin. On Bligh's death in 1817 he wrote that there had been 'no settled system of tyranny' aboard the *Providence*, but made frequent references to 'those violent tornadoes of temper when he lost himself', 'the unbridled licence of his power of speech'.

By contrast, the only complainant against Christian

would appear to have been Bligh himself, and then in a heavily-edited manuscript written *after* the mutiny. Clearly we must seek the causes of the mutiny in events that occurred aboard the *Bounty* on its ill-starred voyage which began on 23 December 1787.

VOYAGE TO TAHITI. A howling, persistent wind blowing from the North Sea down the English Channel carried the *Bounty* away from the shores she would never see again. Its savage coldness made the eyes of the ratings water and all but skinned alive the little group of midshipmen huddled on deck.

The crew, apart from Bligh, included forty-four men. In addition, on the advice of Sir Joseph Banks, President of the Royal Society, two botanists were aboard. They were David Nelson and William Brown. Sir Joseph had made all the arrangements for the journey and Lord Sydney, a Secretary of State, had secured from 'the farmer King' George III, Bligh's orders and warrant.

The American War of Independence had cut off the main source of food for the islands of the West Indies. It was advisable that they should become more self-sufficient. The Royal Society had offered its gold Medal to anyone who could succeed in conveying a minimum of 'six bread-fruit plants . . . in a growing state' from the Pacific Islands to the West Indies.

Bligh's orders read: 'Whereas the King, upon a representation from the merchants and planters, interested in His Majesty's West India possessions, that the introduction of the bread-fruit tree into the islands of those seas, to constitute an article of food, would be of very essential benefit to the inhabitants, have, in order to promote the interests of so respectable body of his subjects (especially in an instance which promises general advantage) thought fit that measures should be taken for the procuring of some of these trees and conveying them to the said West India islands: and whereas the vessel under your command hath, in consequence thereof, been stored and victualled for that service, and fitted with proper conveniences and necessaries for the preservation of as many of the said trees as, for her size, can be taken on board her. . . . You are, therefore, in pursuance of His Majesty's pleasure, signified to us by Lord Sydney, one of his principle secretaries of state, hereby required to put to sea in the vessel you command, the first favourable opportunity of wind and weather, and proceed with her as expeditiously as possible round Cape Horn to the Society Islands, situate in the Southern Ocean in the latitude of about 18 degrees south, and longitude of about 210 degrees east from Greenwich. . . .' The bread-fruit trees were to be off-loaded 'at His Majesty's botanical gardens at St. Vincent, for the benefit of the Windward Islands'. From there they were to proceed to Jamaica, and from there make their return to England.

Bligh, whom the crew were to nickname 'Old Bread-fruit', wrote in his log: 'The great cabin was appropriated for the preservation of the plants, and extended as far forward as the after hatchway. It had two large skylights, and on each side three skuttles for air, and was fitted with a false floor cut full of holes to contain the garden pots in which the plants were to be brought home. The deck was covered with lead, and at the foremost corners of the cabin were fixed pipes to carry off the water that drained from the plants into tubs placed below to save it for future use.'

Nickname notwithstanding, it was not the 'greenhouse operation' side of the *Bounty*'s mission that excited Bligh most. He had caught from Cook an enthusiasm for exploration and map-making. And the expedition's sponsor, Sir Joseph Banks, had told him 'to explore and survey' the relatively unfrequented regions of the Pacific between Tahiti and Timoa. In short, to complete Captain Cook's work. For this reason Bligh carried with him a strong sense of historic mission.

He would have been devastated had he known that the Admiralty had forgotten about him before he was out of the Channel. And he *was* devastated when, after his courageous 3,900-mile voyage in the *Bounty*'s launch with an acrimonious crew, he caught ship to an England in which his exploits were almost totally eclipsed by events in revolutionary France.

But as he caught the first grey of daylight over the Bay of Biscay, Christmas day 1787, History was his companion and Destiny his spur.

The 'strong gale and heavy weather' which had swept them out of the Channel, abated and enabled Bligh's crew to keep a cheerful Christmas. But by 29 December they were thrown by a strong easterly; severe damage was done to the ship's rigging, casks of beer lashed to the deck broke loose and were washed overboard and the ship's boats were badly damaged. When it became clear that a large quantity of food had been rendered useless and that 'the sea had stove in our stern and filled the cabin with water' the decision was taken to put in at Tenerife. There Bligh, on 4 January 1788, selected Christian – rather than Fryer, Peckover or Elphinstone – to represent him before the island's governor and make request for the necessary provisions and permission to refit in harbour.

On 10 January the *Bounty* sailed out of Tenerife. Everyone was put on two-thirds of the usual allowance of bread. Within days they were caught up in the south-east trade wind. 'We had much wet weather,' wrote Bligh in his log, 'the air close and sultry.' The rain fell so heavily that they caught 700 gallons of water. The rains continued for weeks. The persistent wet weather, combined with 'the closeness of the air' 'covered everything with mildew'.

By early March they were 100 leagues from the coast of Brazil. They caught and ate a shark and five dolphins. 'I gave orders for (the crew's) light tropical clothing to be put by, and made them dress in a manner more suited to a cold climate', noted Bligh as they sailed deeper into the southern hemisphere towards the Straits of Magellan.

By mid-March they had entered 'thick foggy weather' and 'saw whales and albatrosses'. On 24 March they entered the dreaded Straits. Almost immediately they encountered a 'heavy gale'. 'At 6 in the morning the storm exceeded what I have ever met with before,' noted

Bligh, 'and the sea, from the frequent shifting of the wind, running in contrary directions, broke exceeding hard. . . . The gale continued, with severe squalls of hail and sleet. . . .'

On 12 April the situation had not improved. The ship began to complain. Every available man was on the pumps. 'The decks became so leaky that I was obliged to alot the great cabin (the one left vacant for the bread-fruit) . . . , to those people who had wet berths, to hang their hammocks in, and by this means the between deck was less crowded.' For days at a time they drifted before the wind. By 9 May they had been driven so far off course that they considered putting in at the Falkland Islands. However, 'I did not think it worth while to stop at these islands, as the refreshment we might obtain there would scarce repay us for the expense of time.'

Bligh, to whom Glynn Christian gives credit for paying unusual attention to the seamen's health, comfort and hygiene, took an important decision: to cross the South Atlantic from Cape Horn to the Cape of Good Hope. 'My people', wrote Bligh, 'were getting ill, and I had the honour to have the most discretionary orders to do as I thought best for the good of the voyage.' On 24 May they anchored at the Cape of Good Hope and remained there until 1 July 1788. This time a more substantial refit was carried out on the *Bounty* which was also reprovisioned.

They sailed due east. By 19 September, 'after having passed the south part of New Zealand', Bligh rejoiced that he was once more on course for Tahiti. On 26 October they anchored at Matavai Bay. 'A great number of canoes came off to us', wrote Bligh. As soon as the islanders had ascertained that the crew 'were from Britain and not from Lima they crowded on board in vast numbers, notwithstanding our endeavours to prevent it'.

They had reached the island of bread-fruit. But it was not bread-fruit the crew had in mind as they waded ashore. . . .

ISLAND IN THE SUN

TAHITI. James Morrison, bo'sun's mate (who kept his own record of events), back-flipped off the gunwale. He found himself down among huge, glimmering schools of fish. The colours and shapes were remarkable and the sensation of slicing through the sun-laced waters made him think of heaven.

The Tahitians had held Captain Cook in high regard. The *Bounty*'s arrival at Matavai Bay was the cause of great rejoicing. Tokens of friendship were received by those who had waded ashore.

Fletcher Christian came ashore in the cutter. He made contact with the local chief, presented him with gifts 'from King George' and, on King George's behalf, invited him on board the *Bounty*.

The Matavai chief, his family and retinue, came out in a flotilla of canoes. Tinah (the chief's name) treated Bligh with such deference that he might have been Captain Cook or even King George III himself. Aware of the requirements of Tahitian etiquette, Bligh readily 'joined noses' with the chief and his wife. 'The King and all the royal family', as Bligh persisted in calling them, were given a conducted tour of the ship. 'The King', in particular, was fascinated by the *Bounty*, and virtually turned over the captain's cabin in his enthusiasm. Soon Bligh became aware that the chief's party had accumulated so many mementoes that he had more than paid in kind for the 'large hog and some bread-fruit' which had been the chief's gifts to him.

The Matavai chief showed no inclination to leave. When he had ascertained through the, at this stage, limited communication system between himself and Bligh, what the cannons were for, he insisted that one be fired. Bligh obliged. That evening he gave a great dinner party for the chief and his entire retinue. Thereafter, he wrote, 'the King and all the royal family were always my guests'. Bligh was in his element.

The chief, noted Bligh, 'was fed by one of his attendants, who sat by him for that purpose, this being a particular custom among some of the superior chiefs. I must do him the justice to say he kept his attendant constantly employed. There was, indeed, little reason to complain of want of appetite in any of my guests.'

The following morning, perhaps aware of the extent to which they had depleted the *Bounty*'s supplies, Chief Tinah sent canoe-loads of pigs to the *Bounty* for salting. There was also the invitation that Bligh should do him the honour of a return visit. That evening a marvellous beach party, in Bligh's honour, was organized in Matavai Bay. Mindful of the role he must fill as a Great Man – Captain Cook's successor – Bligh rose to the occasion. He took notice of the hoards of children around him. When it became obvious that he was making presents of beads only to the babes in arms, boys of 10 and 12 years old were 'caught up in arms and brought to me'. This, said Bligh, 'created much laughter'. The captain gave himself the credit of having coped with the whole evening 'with much drollery and good humour'. Nevertheless, when he returned to his cabin on the *Bounty* well after midnight he realized he was right out of the gifts and trinkets he had brought with him to make an impression on the natives. Next day he felt a tremendous confidence about the whole venture; 'the object of my mission would probably be accomplished with ease'.

BREAD-FRUIT. Bligh had been careful to inform the crew that none of the islanders was to be told the purpose of his venture. He need hardly have bothered; their minds were on other things. He felt that if they became aware that there was a premium on bread-fruit the price might suddenly increase!

Soon Bligh was touring the entire island and encountering other chieftains. His object: to find the best specimens of the bread-fruit trees. His method was to present the chieftains with gifts as if they came directly from King George, whose name was familiar to them from Captain Cook's visits. Bligh would then ask, 'Will not you send something to King George in return?' They invariably replied in the affirmative, offering the most valuable articles they could think of, to be told that King George was only interested in bread-fruit trees!

As the bread-fruit specimens were accumulated it was Mr. Christian's job to erect tents on shore 'for the lodgement of the plants'. He did so with the co-operation of the two botanists. Following Cook's example Bligh endeavoured to cultivate a garden in a sheltered spot near Matavai Bay. With the encouragement of his sponsor he had brought a variety of seeds with him. The garden was planted with melon, cucumber and a selection of English vegetables. The islanders seemed a little puzzled when they were told that these were to be for their use.

Bligh was the toast of the entire island. Each evening was caught up with social events. If he was not entertaining the chieftains and their families aboard the *Bounty*, then they were entertaining him ashore. One evening they accorded him what he clearly believed was the ultimate accolade. He was, himself, made an honorary chief; a 'piece of cloth' was 'put over my shoulders and round my waist in the manner of the chiefs'. Bligh was fairly bursting with pride.

'EVERY MAN HIS OWN TYO . . .' While Bligh played the role of the Great Man from a Distant Land the crewmen were otherwise engaged; chiefly among the trees, in the shadows. 'An intimacy between the natives and our people', noted Bligh, developed almost immediately after the arrival of the *Bounty*. 'There was scarce a man in the ship who had not his *tyo* or friend.' Bligh neither disapproved nor was particularly interested.

Among the Polynesians the behaviour of neither the girls nor the crewmen occasioned comment. Tensions arising from sexual encounters were few at first. While the Tahitian girls were by no means the half-dressed, grass-

28

skirted temptresses of contemporary line drawings, it is clear that they took the initiative in the earlier sexual encounters. In the main these encounters were promiscuous and short-term. The main exception to this was Christian himself. He early settled down into blissful domesticity with a statuesque beauty he called Isabella.

The only other seamen who developed 'strong connections' with the native girls – that is, relationships which were more or less monagamous – were John Adams (Alexander Smith) and Quintal. Hence at least three women on the island regarded themselves as being in a permanent sense 'married' to their partners.

The southern hemisphere summer of 1788-89 was paradisal for the officers and ratings of *Bounty* – and for Bligh who was deriving equal pleasure from his social rounds.

Only very occasionally would something occur to disrupt the calm of the sun-drenched, carefree life of the island which had so easily assimilated the crew of the British vessel. But Bligh's roar struck terror into the islanders, including the chieftains. It was at this time that the officers and crew of the *Bounty*, who have left their accounts to posterity, first became aware that Fletcher Christian was being singled out by Bligh for public humiliation.

Petty thefts had been committed by the islanders from the time of *Bounty*'s arrival. However, when the rudder of the large cutter was stolen – presumably with great difficulty – Bligh decided that it was time to make someone an example. First he blamed his officers in general, and Christian in particular, for negligence. When the culprit was found he was given a dozen lashes. This, in Bligh's words, 'Did no more than interrupt the good terms on which we were with the chiefs'. It was, perhaps, to mellow his honoured guest's humour that Tinah, that evening, organized a special dance for Bligh's benefit. He must have been relieved that the temper tantrums displayed earlier in the day did not inhibit the captain's enjoyment of the half-hour dance which 'consisted of wanton gestures and motions' – and was followed by a women's wrestling match!

The second interruption of the island's calm was the not-altogether unexpected death of Huggan, the ship's surgeon. John Huggan had been the only crew member of whom Bligh had complained before the *Bounty* left port: 'His indolence and corpulence render him rather unfit for the voyage.' For once Bligh had been understating his case. It is clear that Huggan was an alcoholic and was inebriated for the greater part of the time. His death, said Bligh, was 'the effect of intemperance and indolence'. 'Intemperance' would probably have covered it. The obese Huggan was buried on shore on 10 December 1788.

It was on the day of his funeral that the rumour spread among the islanders that the *Bounty* was about to sail. Panic set in in some quarters when, on 24 December, they noticed that Fletcher Christian, with botanist David Nelson, was organizing the removal of the 774 plants thus far acquired from the tents on shore to the *Bounty*. In fact it was a false alarm. Bligh had been concerned that the high seas which occasionally whipped Matavai Bay to a frenzy might endanger the *Bounty*. The day after she sailed out of the bay, *Bounty* was successfully navigated into a safer anchorage in a neighbouring bay. For the time being life on the island paradise could continue.

DESERTION. Bligh's major crisis began on 5 January 1789. Christian's watch began at 4am. As soon as he came on duty he realized that the small cutter was missing and reported the fact to Bligh.

Immediately the entire ship's company was mustered.

Three men were found to be absent: Charles Churchill, William Muspratt and John Millward.

After a brief search it was discovered that they had taken with them arms and ammunition.

Islanders came forward with the information that the deserters had been seen with the cutter in Matavai Bay and that they had departed from there in a canoe for the island of Tethuroa.

By mid-morning five islanders had recovered the cutter, to Bligh's satisfaction. But his anger was unabated; he expressed his determination not to leave Tahiti before the deserters had been found and punished.

On 13 January a party of islanders left in canoes for the island to which the deserters had gone, with a view to capturing them. But it was nine days before Bligh received news of the whereabouts of the deserters. He then put out in the cutter fully armed, ready for a shoot-out. In the event they surrendered without a fight. Bligh noted that they had had no alternative since their ammunition was wet and the islanders hostile. His account is contradicted by others; the deserters had, in fact, been captured by the islanders who had persuaded them to give themselves up.... This did nothing to mitigate their circumstances. Bligh ordered that they be given a flogging.

TENSIONS. As the tropical summer wore on, the hedonistic pleasures of the crewmen began to pall and, more significantly, to lead to tensions and violence.

One man was detected with a married woman by her husband. He was stabbed in the belly with a knife. 'Fortunately', wrote Bligh, 'the intestines escaped and the wound did not prove dangerous.'

On another occasion a girl who had lived more-or-less consistently with the coxswain was found to have beaten another girl half to death who had become a rival for his affections.

As a result of another domestic crisis, seaman Isaac Martin was given nineteen lashes for striking an islander.

Throughout all, relationships between Bligh and Chief Tinah had remained good. Arrangements were afoot for the local chief and his family to visit England. Even when islanders were taken on board and flogged for petty theft, the chieftain's regard for Bligh remained undiminished.

However, on one occasion the repercussions of Bligh's temper trantrum almost made an enemy of Tinah. One of the cables of the *Bounty* was discovered to have been partially severed. Bligh's rage was so awesome that the villagers living in the vicinity of *Bounty*, including the parents of Tinah, made for the mountains! When Bligh came to write his narrative months later the mutiny was past and he chose to interpret this incident as the first indication of mutinous behaviour; by then he had convinced himself that the object had been to send the *Bounty* out to sea.

All were aware that the unreal life on Tahiti must sooner or later come to an end. By early March 1789 preparations began for the final departure. On 27 March, superintended by Fletcher Christian, the last of the 1,015 bread-fruit plants had been transported to the ship and placed (in their pots) in the sockets specially made for them in the great cabin. In addition to the bread-fruit other varieties of plants had been taken.

They had been on Tahiti for twenty-three weeks. Bligh's only comment upon departure on 3 April: 'We left Tahiti with only two patients in the venereal list, which shows that the disease has not gained ground.' One or two of the crewmen had been seen saying fond farewells to the island. Christian had been seen, alone, atop the great cliff, the sea below singing hoarsely to itself.

With every man on board Morrison recorded that 'everybody seemed in high spirits' on leaving Tahiti. The major objective of the voyage had been achieved. This was the first leg of their voyage home; and, wrote Morrison, 'the talk was all of home'. A course was set for the island of Tofua. 'The weather became squally', wrote Bligh, 'and a body of thick black clouds collected in the east.'

With Tahiti receding in the distance Fletcher Christian looked up at the clouds which packed in great, alarming haste across the night sky. It is unlikely that he was thinking of England and home.

This is the Pitcairn thousands of visitors have seen since the mutineer's hideaway was first discovered in 1809 — twenty years after their arrival.

The island as the famished mutineers first saw it, emerging out of the sea mist.

Pitcairn's economy still relies heavily on the turbulent, often violent and cruel sea that roars at the cliffs.

PRELUDE TO MUTINY

CAUSES. On 13 October 1789 (from Batavia following the terrifying journey in *Bounty*'s launch) Bligh wrote this in a letter to Sir Joseph Banks: 'I can only conjecture that the buccaneers ... have ideally assured themselves of a more happy life among the Tahitians than they could possibly have in England, which, joined to some female connections, has most likely been the leading cause of the whole business.'

A document drawn up by Bligh was read out before a court martial on 12 August 1792. In it he alleged that, while he was tied to the mizzen mast at the height of the mutiny, 'the mutineers expressed much joy that they would soon see Tahiti'. This deposition was written at Coupang on 18 August 1789.

Clearly Bligh's original intention, before he ascertained the actual course taken by the mutineers, was to explain the mutiny in terms of the sex-drive of undisciplined men. Later, with more facts at his disposal, he would shift his ground; complaining about the poor quality of his officers and their failure to control the ratings.

Fletcher Christian's apologists have attempted to explain the mutiny in terms of Bligh's undue severity and fondness for the lash. However, based on recent research at the Mitchell Library, Sydney, Glynn Christian has reached the view that Bligh was by no means cruel, that he did not flog unmercifully, and that he might even have been 'far too lenient' (by comparison, certainly, with his mentor Captain Cook or with Fletcher Christian following the mutiny).

Naval historians, like Richard Hough, have endeavoured to explain the mutiny entirely in terms of a series of events which led to a build-up of tension aboard the *Bounty* in the three-week period between her departure from Tahiti and the day of the mutiny. Certainly there is much to commend this latter view. But it is likely that it does not represent the whole story. . . .

THE BEGINNING OF SORROWS. If Fletcher Christian was in an uncharacteristically morose humour as the *Bounty* sailed away from Tahiti, the leaving of Isabella – nicknamed 'Mainmast' by his fellow crew members – was not the complete explanation.

John Adams was witness to a major quarrel between Bligh and Christian at Cape Town months before. Prior to that quarrel Bligh had reposed more confidence in the master's mate – whom he had asked to assume the rank of lieutenant over the head of the master – than in any other man aboard. After Cape Town, Adams maintained, the 'original quarrel' was, to a greater or lesser degree, 'kept up until the mutiny'.

This rift arose, according to Glynn Christian, from the fact that Fletcher Christian was under obligation to Bligh for financial reasons. The famous mutineer's descendant has found evidence among Bligh's papers in the Mitchell Library that Fletcher Christian had borrowed money from Bligh.

Given Bligh's vindictiveness, attested to by a score of witnesses in courts martial in that part of his career following the *Bounty* débâcle, it was well within his character to use Christian's indebtedness to make him squirm. Christian, after all, had been taken on at the Captain's discretion, because his family was bankrupt. . . .

In Bligh's own narrative of the mutiny he admitted to having reminded Christian of how much he owed to his captain. Christian had displayed visible embarrassment. 'That – Captain Bligh – that is the thing. I am in hell – I am in hell.' That had been Bligh's parting shot as the launch pulled away. . . .

An unpaid debt may also help to explain what John Fryer professed to find so puzzling when he made his sworn statement before the court martial in 1792. Why did Christian so resolutely resist the pressures placed on him by the other mutineers to treat Captain Bligh

34

a great deal more roughly than he was treated?

'SEEPING MADNESS . . .'   Bligh's public humiliations of Christian began on Tahiti. The first came after the thefts. The second with the accusation that Christian had connived at the flight of the deserters. Deep wounds were left in Christian's ego. Bligh had used words he found it difficult to forgive. It must have crossed his mind that the captain, who so evidently found Polynesian promiscuity utterly perplexing, resented his relationship with Isabella.

But things became infinitely worse when the men, who had enjoyed many weeks of untrammelled freedom on Tahiti, were once again in the tight confines of the *Bounty*. As the vessel threaded its way through the islands of the South Pacific a kind of seeping madness began to ooze through the ship.

The *Bounty* sailed through day after day of dark, lowering weather with lightning, thunder and tropical downpours. When the captain was in range the air fairly crackled with venom and vituperation.

Purcell and Fryer had been victimized earlier and were not exempt now. But increasingly Christian bore the brunt of Bligh's paranoid rage. Before Cape Town there had been a 'special relationship' between Christian and his captain. Since then a steady deterioration. Now in the fetid dampness of a cramped vessel, even when no words were exchanged, it seemed that Christian was the subject of a seething, inchoate rage. At last it began to seem to some that the seeping madness which had crept into Bligh's brain had infected Christian too and, to a lesser degree, *all* the officers.

Tahitian days had been spacious, slow and quiet, merging into one another. Every man on board *Bounty* was now suffering a severe reaction to the rigours of life on a small vessel now cluttered with plant life, her decks an obstacle course of coconut heaps and pens containing noisy hogs (*all* somebody's property, gifts from the islanders).

Bligh was to charge his officers with indolence, incompetence and worse. In fact he may have been externalizing his own guilt: he had allowed his men to become dissolute and undisciplined during the months on Tahiti. The *Bounty* needed the re-imposition of a strong hand, but not a high hand; a strong hand applied evenly, not with abuse, threats or histrionics.

RATIONS CUT. Bligh's instinct told him to pile on the discipline and cut down on the rations. The men were limited to a ration of pork and six plantains a day on a vessel groaning under the weight of fresh fruit and vegetables, salted pork and various delicacies brought off the island. The newly-reduced ration, barely sufficient to support life, and the sheer irrationality of it all made Bligh's discipline seem insane and ridiculous.

Bligh reinstated daily inspections for cleanliness, found most men wanting – and stopped the grog for the entire crew. John Sumner received twelve lashes for no reason that he could understand. Bligh repeatedly cursed his second-in-command in front of the crew for supposed failures. On one occasion Christian replied: 'Sir, your abuse is so bad that I cannot do my duty with any pleasure.' On a daily basis Bligh rounded on his officers calling them 'scoundrels, damned rascals, hounds, hell hounds, beasts, and infamous wretches'.

A new island was discovered. Two days and nights were spent there while Bligh charted its coastline. Trade with the islanders began – but Bligh gave orders to sail just as arrangements had been made to get women aboard.

For long periods Fletcher Christian drew away, closed in a violent silence.

TENSION BUILDING. Nerve-stretching stress affected the entire crew. There was a general feeling that something would have to give.

Set against the westering sun the island of Nomuka was sighted. Bligh gave orders to heave to. He wanted to finish some map drawing left undone from his voyage with Cook.

Bligh went ashore with presents for the island chiefs – but received only another mountain of coconuts in return. An historic gift, as events were to turn out.

The mood of the islanders was uncertain, their eyes giving a different message from their smiles. Christian was blamed when the bow anchor went missing. There were a few taut moments of silence as he glared evenly into the captain's eyes.

On 26 April, two days before the mutiny, two parties were put ashore on Nomuka, one headed by Christian, the other headed by Elphinstone. Christian and his party of eleven had orders to fill the two launches with as many casks of water as they would hold. Elphinstone, with his four men, was ordered to fell timber. Bligh ordered both parties to take arms with them – but not to use them. The arms were to be left in the launches.

The clouds were low and threatening. It was a thoroughly nasty day, spitting with rain.

Long before the launches came ashore a large crowd had gathered. It was difficult to measure their mood. But there was enough in their demeanour to indicate that what had brought them there was more than curiosity.

When Christian's party landed the sullen islanders tried to take the empty casks by force. They became insistent and menacing. Christian decided that it would be folly to follow orders and leave the arms in the launches.

No sooner was his party organized, carrying both casks and armaments, than the wisdom of his decision became evident. It became obvious to everyone that the islanders were in a warlike mood. Spears were thrown and narrowly missed their targets. Christian replied with muskets.

The whole expedition which involved many journeys between the inland fresh-water source and the launches was fraught with danger. Some men were detailed to carry the casks, others to guard them. Warlike islanders shadowed the party throughout.

Against all the odds, Christian managed to bring off two launch-loads of filled casks.

Elphinstone's party had had more limited success and

were obliged to report the theft, by the islanders, of the cooper's adze.

Bligh had a face, and a voice, like thunder. In full view and full hearing of the entire crew he roared at Christian: 'You damned cowardly rascal! Are you afraid of a set of natives while you have arms to defend yourselves?'

Christian stood still and for a moment was silent.

Patiently he began a detailed explanation to Bligh of what had happened and why the use of muskets had been necessary. Bligh refused to listen and shook his fist in Christian's face.

Fryer, the master, had been in Christian's party. He had seen what had happened. Had not been able to understand Bligh's original order that the armaments should be left unguarded in the launches. Was Bligh deliberately creating a situation in which he could humiliate Christian? It had not escaped the master's notice that the ritual humiliation of Fletcher Christian occurred now on a daily basis. Fryer himself had come very near to being clubbed to death on the island. He did his best now to back Christian's testimony. But Bligh interrupted, refused to listen and raged on.

He berated all the men in Christian's party and went so far as to grab McKoy by the collar and aim a pistol at his head – and to threaten to blow his brains out.

'WHEN WE REACH ENDEAVOUR STRAITS . . . ' The captain's response to the theft of the adze was to keep as hostage four elderly chieftains who had come aboard the *Bounty*. They would be kept until the adze was returned, he announced.

But the old chieftains were terrified, and had no idea what the stranger was trying to achieve. Nor had the vast crowd which had gathered along the shoreline. Thirty-six hours before the mutiny began, Bligh was obliged to return the chieftains and admit failure.

He was at odds with the entire crew. As he had done once before, he threatened that, when the *Bounty* reached Endeavour Straits, 'he would kill one half of the people, make the officers jump overboard and would make them eat grass like cows'. In a number of the sworn statements taken by Professor Edward Christian at the time of the courts martial, mention was made that the entire crew was in terror of their arrival at Endeavour Straits. One testimony asserted that master's mate Christian and midshipman Stewart, in particular, feared that in some way the captain would make an end of them when they had reached the Straits.

The night of 26 to 27 April was a restless one. Thunder rumbled. The air was unbearably humid.

THE DAY BEFORE. On the 27th Bligh uncharacteristically remained below in his cabin until noon. It is difficult to guess at his state of mind, but clearly he was working himself up into a state of advanced paranoia.

Fletcher Christian too was reported to be withdrawn and depressed, discharging his duties in a daze.

When the captain eventually came on deck he strolled straight up to Christian and roared: 'Damn your blood, you have stolen my coconuts!'

The situation was ridiculous on the deck of a ship at sea littered with heaps of rolling coconuts.

But nobody laughed.

Bligh was referring to the heap of coconuts which he had received as a gift the previous day.

Fryer intervened. Taking the captain entirely seriously – he knew better than to do otherwise – he expressed the view that the heap had been pressed close from being run over by the men in the night. Crew members like Morrison who had kept their sense of perspective looked around at the deck littered with heaps of coconuts and fruit, caged hogs and chickens. He could scarcely believe what he was hearing.

Humbly Christian answered his captain: 'I was dry; I thought it of no consequence. I took only one, and I am sure no one touched another.'

Again, shaking his fist in the face of his second-in-command, Bligh roared: 'You lie, you scoundrel, you have stolen one half.'

Christian appeared much hurt and agitated. In a low voice he answered: 'Why do you treat me thus, Captain Bligh?'

As an onlooker testified at a later date: 'Captain Bligh then shook his hand in his face and said, "No reply", and called him a thief and other abusive names. . . . The captain then called all hands upon deck, and desired "the people to look after the officers, and the officers to look after the people, as if there never were such a set of damned thieving rascals under any man's command in the world before".'

Shrieking, Bligh next accused Edward Young. Then he turned from man to man until every one of the ship's company had been interrogated. 'I suppose you will steal my yams next', he growled. 'But I'll sweat you for it, you rascal. I'll look after you for a bit longer for my own good, but I'll make half of you jump overboard before you get through Endeavour Straits. You may all go to hell!'

There was that sinister threat again. All heard it.

To his clerk, Bligh said: 'Stop these villains' grog, Mr. Samuel, and give them but half a pound of yams tomorrow. If they go on stealing I'll reduce the allowance to a quarter pound.' Then he turned abruptly and went back to his cabin.

For a time there was silence. Everyone looked at everyone else for a response. It occurred to some of the officers – as it was to occur to officers under Bligh's command on future voyages – that their captain was temporarily insane.

About 4pm Bligh surfaced again. Again he abused Christian. This time the substance of what he had to say was not overheard.

Christian was weeping copiously when he left Bligh. Purcell, the carpenter, was alarmed. He had never seen Christian like this before. Unaware of Bligh's latest accusation he said to Christian, 'What is the matter, Mr. Christian?'

Christian replied: 'Can you ask me and hear the treatment I receive?'

Purcell replied, 'Do not I receive as bad as you do?'

Christian said, 'You have something to protect you, and can speak again; but if I should speak to him as you do, he would probably break me, turn me before the mast, and perhaps flog me; and if he did, it would be the death of us both, for I'm sure that I should take him in my arms and jump overboard with him.'

This was a telling comment. Though second-in-command, Fletcher Christian was not a warrant officer. The only officer on board holding the King's commission was Bligh himself. The King's warrant had been held by Huggan (now dead), Fryer the master, Cole the bo'sun, Peckover the gunner and Purcell the carpenter. Christian, like the other officers, was in effect a petty officer with limited privileges. He was classed with the ratings, and could therefore be flogged. What he had told the carpenter was: There is no limit to the humiliations to which Bligh can subject me.

Coming close on the heels of a *sotto voce* threat from Bligh to Christian this comment, in all probability, indicates that Christian had just received the threat of a flogging for his theft of one coconut.

In this atmosphere *anything* could happen – and probably would. Purcell, also much abused by Bligh, was at least a warrant officer with a warrant officer's privileges. Christian was deeply regretting the terms on which he had come aboard; almost certainly he had just been threatened with the ultimate humiliation.

In the hearing of most of the officers and many of the ratings he said, 'I would rather die ten thousand deaths than bear this treatment. I always do my duty as an officer and as a man ought to do, yet I receive this scandalous usage.'

Purcell was later to testify that he had never seen Christian in tears before and to affirm: 'He was no milk sop.'

Morrison wrote: 'The officers then got together and were heard to murmur much at their treatment.'

The next time Christian had occasion to speak to Purcell it was later in the evening and the sun had set. He was asking for materials which Purcell was sure he was about to use to make a raft on which to escape from his impossible situation. The rumour began to spread that the second-in-command was contemplating suicide.

After all that had occurred Bligh nevertheless had the effrontery to send his servant to ask Christian to dine with him that evening. Politely Christian made his excuses. The other officers had made an agreement that, if asked, they would refuse to take Christian's place.

The servant returned: 'Would *anyone* care to sup with their captain?' In turn they all refused.

Then Tom Hayward, all jug ears and scalding sincerity, told the servant that he would be glad to accept.

He left to the boos and hisses of his fellow midshipmen.

It was the evening of 27 April. HMS *Bounty* was just thirty miles off Tofua, one of the inaptly-named Friendly Islands. The night was humid and oppressive. Though contemplating desertion, however, Christian was still not contemplating mutiny.

IN SEARCH OF PARADISE

BACK TO TAHITI. Guilt plagued Fletcher Christian's mind and showed in his face as Bligh and his nineteen loyal men pulled away in the launch. What chance had they in the twenty-three foot launch across the 3,600 miles between Tofua and Timor? He could not have predicted that they would take on more supplies from Tofua and, on an ounce of bread and a gill of water a day, successfully navigate that little-known sea.

Perhaps Bligh's crossing to Timor was the real epic. But it is not what has captured the popular imagination ever since.

Aboard the *Bounty* Christian, after a few hours of decisive leadership in the mutiny, now withdrew again into the gloom which had characterized his behaviour for three weeks past. It seemed that his head was in a cloud of his own private weather; that his mind was at least as tortured as before.

His mood clashed violently with that of his shipmates, exulting in their new-found freedom and – they believed – licence.

Coleman, Norman, McIntosh and Stewart were confused and had mixed feelings. They had been detained on the *Bounty* against their will. They feared for the future, aware that Fryer's prediction was all too accurate. Wherever they should choose to hide, the Royal Navy would find them, try them and hang them. In the day of retribution, would a court martial allow for the fact that they had taken no active part in the mutiny? Or would they merely be treated like the rest because they were found with them?

Christian was also aware that Fryer's prediction could be expected to come true. He found himself wondering how long they had. Weeks? Months? Was it possible to find an island hideaway, remote, sparsely populated, without a harbour, where they could scuttle the ship and be lost to history?

He looked at the riotous crewmen and shuddered for the disgrace he would bring to his family if taken with them and returned to the homeland.

Pressed, he denied that, in Bligh's absence, he could now be considered captain. 'I have no right to command you and will act in any station I am assigned to.'

The mutineers were puzzled by his attitude.

Somebody had the idea of *electing* a captain.

Christian was elected unanimously.

Since Tahiti, Christian had been aware of the need for calm, even-handed discipline. This rabble who had been allowed to run wild, run free, needed a firm hand. He informed them that he would be providing that firm hand and that some of his friends might well be in for a surprise.

And so they were.

In the weeks that followed, Fletcher Christian enforced a more rigid discipline than the *Bounty* crew had known since they left Spithead. But the discipline was rational, fair – and they accepted it.

Christian's discipline had but one eccentric feature. Thousands of miles from home (and never likely to see home as free men again), and after a mutiny, he decided to enforce the wearing of uniforms. Men were set to work to make uniforms from the *Bounty*'s spare studding sails. The wearing of a uniform, albeit a slightly comic and ill-fitting one, had a positive effect on the company's morale.

To provide them with more room to move many (though by no means all) of the plants were removed from the great cabin and hurled into the sea.

Now, with his crew of twenty-five (instead of forty-four), aware that at least four men were loyal to him under duress, and that an unknown additional number would prefer to take their chances with an English court martial rather than be part of the scheme he was beginning to evolve in his mind, Fletcher Christian wondered what should be his next move. He worked under the assumption that he had weeks, rather than months in which to find his island hideaway.

Sails were trimmed, the course altered – for a return to Tahiti.

Many a man's heart lifted as he saw the sweeping shoulder of high, empty land, beyond which was Matavai Bay.

At this stage Christian did not think it prudent to allow any man the option of remaining on Tahiti. Tahiti, after all, would be the first place where the Royal Navy would look for the mutineers.

First to the beaches where the cutter ran aground were Jenny, Mary, Sarah and Isabella who regarded themselves as the wives of Adams, McIntosh, Quintal and Christian respectively.

The four women were taken aboard. In addition, seventeen males and one young girl came aboard. Only by trickery did they manage to lure an additional seven women at the last minute, sailing with them against their will.

The whole operation was carried out in a hurry. Christian feared that the chiefs would turn hostile when they learned of the truth of the mutiny, and feared that the stories he had told to account for the absence of Bligh had not been believed.

Now began in earnest the search for the island hideaway among the thousand or more islands of the Pacific.

The first island chosen was Tubuai. Almost immediately the project began to look unpromising. The islanders were hostile. Grapeshot was used on attacking canoes before the mutineers could even land.

There was a feeling from the start that the venture would not work out. Nevertheless, a sense of something near desperation led Christian and his closest henchmen to continue.

Raised ground was selected on which to build a fortification. The green sea broke upon the narrow beach with a hollow sound, followed by the sharp hiss of withdrawal. Despite reservations, Christian believed that at least this would be a defensible position. Based on plans that he himself had drawn up, the company began to construct Fort George.

But Fort George was never completed. The islanders had been cowed by the use of grapeshot but, as the days went by, they showed more and more signs of open aggession. In addition, there were tensions within the group of mutineers. The shortage of women was the major source of conflict.

Within a few weeks of their mutiny, the mutineers found themselves fighting a colonial war of sorts. Sixty-six islanders were killed and two Englishmen injured.

It was clear to all that the Tubuai venture had been a failure and that they had best cut their losses. The decision was taken to go back to the *Bounty*. In the men's minds there were two choices. One was to return to Tahiti where they would face any fate that might await them; the other was to follow Fletcher Christian's dream of an island fastness lost in the thousand or more islands of the South Pacific where the Royal Navy would never find them.

The alternatives were put to the vote. A majority wanted to return to Tahiti.

'Gentlemen,' said Christian, 'I will carry you and land you wherever you please. I desire no one to stay with me. But I have one favour to request – that you will grant me the ship, tie the foresail and give me a few gallons of water, and leave me to run before the wind, and I shall land upon the first island the ship drives. . . . I will live nowhere where I may be apprehended and brought home to be a disgrace to my family.'

Some felt he was being unnecessarily melodramatic. But Young, as chorus leader to the eight hard-core mutineers, yelled: 'We shall never leave you, Mr. Christian!'

CHRISTIAN'S DREAM.   When they left Tubuai, two islanders came with them.

The *Bounty* arrived at Matavai Bay, Tahiti, for the third and last time on 22 September 1789.

A party went ashore surreptitiously. They soon discov-

46

ered that a Royal Navy frigate, HMS *Mercury*, had already called in. The search was on.

Nevertheless, faced with the alternative fates of following Christian's dream or facing the consequences (if any) of the mutiny, a number of men opted for the latter course.

The first to do so were Stewart, Heywood, Byrne, Coleman, Norman and McIntosh. They asserted that they had taken no part in the mutiny and had nothing to fear. They would, they said, set up home at Matavai until the next British ship arrived to take them home.

The decision of another ten men to remain on Tahiti and risk discovery was rather more surprising. More especially since that group included Churchill, Sumner, Millward, Muspratt, Morrison, Burkett, Hillbrant, Ellison, Skinner and Matt Thompson.

After their taste of Tubuai most of the Tahitian native men also opted to remain.

Before *Bounty* sailed from Tahiti for the last time more women were lured aboard. No sooner had they sailed than it was discovered that a considerable number of these ladies were old and rather stout. Somewhat unchivalrously Christian hove to at the next island and put the old and the overweight ashore in the cutter.

Christian was aware that peace among the remaining crewmen much depended upon male-female relationships being stablilized. He therefore made out a list, matchmaker style, which he believed would minimize friction for the future. Delicate negotiations had to be entered into before the list could be completed. Adams, for example, had to be persuaded to yield his Jenny to Isaac Martin and to accept a new wife. Eventually the list was completed.

Mutineers	*Females*
Christian	Isabella (Mainmast)
Young	Susan
Williams	Pashotu
Quintal	Sarah
Adams	Paurai

McKoy	Mary
Martin	Jenny
Mills	Vahineatua
Brown	Teatuahitea

Tahitians
Talaloo	Nancy
Timoa ⎫	
Nehow ⎬	Mareva
Manalee ⎭	

Tubuaians
Oho ⎫	
Tetaheite ⎭	Tinafanaea

With these somewhat squalid (but essential) details ironed out Christian turned his attention to his charts and instruments. One thought does not seem to have crossed his mind. By treating the Tahitians and Tubuaians as second-class citizens he had created a situation in which, one day, there would be such an eruption of blood that his dream would be all but washed away.

Sails were set for maximum speed. The sky was solid grey but for a thin bar of blue above the low horizon to the west. Towards this they set their course.

The *Bounty* began months of restless voyaging around the Pacific islands. Landings were made, hostile islanders encountered and, repeatedly, hopes abandoned.

As the soft, brief mid-summer dusk of the southern hemisphere began to gather on Christmas day 1789 morale was at an all-time low. Christian's dream of a remote paradise, preferably uninhabited and harbourless, seemed foolish.

Since the mutiny Christian had occupied Bligh's cabin. Here he could be seen poring over his charts, measuring distances between islands, foraging among the papers Bligh had been obliged to leave behind him.

Among these he turned over a copy of Hawkesworth's *Voyages* which had been published in 1773. He looked through the pages of volume 1, following, as he had done on a number of occasions before, the voyage of Cartaret.

BBC TV personality Glynn Christian, descended from the famous mutineer via his second son, examines the grave of John Adams. Adams survived the blood-letting which followed the occupation of Pitcairn by the mutineers. By 1800 he was the only surviving mutineer, patriarch of a rapidly expanding community of women and children. His conversion to Christianity following his discovery of the 'Bounty Bible' caused life on Pitcairn to 'change course' dramatically . . . .

Three generations of a Pitcairn family.

Pitcairn still represents a mix of (old fashioned) English and Polynesian culture. In no area is the Polynesian half of the island's heritage more evident than in diet and the preparation of food.

When he reached page 561 his heart began to thump and his brow to perspire. He read these words: 'We continued our course westward till the evening of 2 July 1767, when we discovered land to the northward of us. Upon approaching it the next day, it appeared like a great rock rising out of the sea; it was not more than five miles in circumference, and seemed to be uninhabited. It was, however, covered with trees . . . and it having been discovered by a young gentleman, son of Major Pitcairn . . . we called it Pitcairn Island.'

This reference was enough to staunch the internal bleeding of Christian's melancholy.

The island named after young Pitcairn contained all the components of Christian's dream. It had isolation. It was, on the evidence of Cartaret, uninhabited. And further to that; Cartaret had seen the surf breaking on the island with such violence that he had not been able to make a landing. Here, surely, was an indication of an island with no harbour. And, as such, the last place where the Royal Navy would look or, if they should decide to look, the last place where they would be able to make a successful landing.

The crew were called together on deck. The announcement was made. Christian was disappointed with its reception. No one said the words, but there was a feeling that they had heard it all before. They did, however, notice the change in their captain. His increased optimism proved catching. In the days of endless ocean that it took to find their island paradise everyone on board came to feel that the whole venture turned on the existence and suitability of the island sighted by young Pitcairn and briefly described by Cartaret.

On 15 January 1790 – nine months after the mutiny – someone shouted, 'Land ahoy!'

They had sailed over 8,000 miles from Tahiti to find an island hideaway. As the shadowy outline of Pitcairn appeared in the blue distance, trepidation must have mixed in with their excitement. On first sighting the island Fletcher Christian's descendant Glynn described it as 'a mile by mile-and-a-half lump of green rock, like a piece of crumpled tissue paper in the middle of nowhere'.

On 18 January, Brown the botanist, Williams, McKoy and Christian, along with three Tahitian men, rode across what would come to be called 'Bounty Bay'. The entire bay was rendered hazardous by half-hidden rocks. It was all but impossible to avoid holing the dilapidated cutter. Eventually they were picked up by one of the vast rollers and, complete with the frail cutter, hurled on to a narrow beach fronted by a 700 foot cliff now called Ship Land Point.

On 23 January 1790 the entire crew – men and women – came ashore on this island, scarcely five miles around, aware that it was their last refuge in a hostile world. Here was home.

Eventually the entire contents of the *Bounty* – pigs, goats and fowls – were ferried ashore in the cutter across the treacherous rocks of the bay, through the mountainous surf. The *Bounty* herself was brought as near to the shore as was possible.

With an eagerness born of long, frustrating, seemingly aimless months at sea, the makings of an island race began taking possession of their promised land.

THE PITCAIRN PARADISE

SETTLEMENT. On the level strip of land above the great cliff there was a thick curtain of banyan trees. Behind these it was decided to construct their settlement. The tree-barrier made them completely invisible from the sea. Hence should any vessel of His Majesty's Navy venture into this unfamiliar expanse of ocean and sight the island they would, with Cartaret, reach the conclusion that it was both uninhabited – and uninhabitable.

The early days on Pitcairn were hard. January was by far the hottest month in the southern summer. During the long hours of daylight, day in and day out, all hands were employed fetching and carrying, filling and emptying the boat as it ferried the last contents across Bounty Bay's surf to the narrow beach. Every time the venture was made it seemed that the men on the cutter put their lives at risk.

When all had been brought ashore the *Bounty* was deliberately run aground on the rocks of Bounty Bay.

Behind the curtain of banyan trees they were building the wooden homes of what is now known as Adamstown.

Almost two centuries after his ancestor Fletcher, Glynn Christian made his own voyage to Pitcairn from Tahiti, aboard a specially chartered schooner. His first impression on seeing the island at a distance was soon to be modified: 'As we sailed along Pitcairn's coast I was amazed at how big it looked and wondered why no one had ever written of the ochre-red earth that showed in great gashes. The cliffs were daunting, aloof, forbidding. Even on this relatively calm morning, I could see enormous spumes of spray as the rollers, unhindered for thousands of miles, crashed into this lonely rock.'

In his description of the Island in *Pitcairn: Children of the Bounty*, I. M. Ball says: 'It was surely . . . a volcanic afterthought. It rises like a green-and-brown iceberg from

51

the blue immensity of the South Pacific, two degrees of latitude below the Tropic of Capricorn and 1,350 miles south-east of Tahiti. It is ringed perpetually with a collar of white, foaming water, and probably has worn that ruff of crushing surf since the cosmic dawn. It was borne from the sea floor in that area where the vastest of all oceans runs out of islands. It qualifies as part of the South Seas, but only just. Between it and the wastes of Antarctica lies hardly a crumb of chartered land. It is among the world's most remote inhabited islands, perhaps the most remote.'

There is no sign today, of course, of the Adamstown built in a hurry by Fletcher Christian and his men in the sweltering heat of the January, February and March of 1790. Glynn Christian provides this description of modern Adamstown: 'Adamstown to the visitor is a continuous puzzle of gardens, half-seen houses, dappled walls, banks of red earth, and the protests of disturbed cocks and hens; it stretches for about half a mile along the north-eastern cliff-top above Bounty Bay, westwards.'

At the centre of Adamstown, says Glynn Christian, is a small paved square edged on three sides by public buildings – the Seventh-day Adventist church, the dispensary, the library, the post office and the court house (in practice used for council meetings and film shows).

Exploring the island Glynn Christian found, as his ancestor must have done before him, the rattling coconut crab and spiders five inches long. . . . Flying above Pitcairn Glynn saw, as Fletcher must have done two centuries before, the flashing white fairy terns and noted too that: 'The muffling effect of a thick foliage quickly absorbs even the incessant surf's thunder.'

Amid this demi-paradise of soft, natural, sub-tropical beauty Christian, Young, Quintal, Adams and the rest set about building a settlement of wooden dwellings surrounded by largish, English-style smallholdings. They quickly realized that the amount of land capable of agricultural development was strictly limited, though the total area of the island was 1,120 acres, or 1.75 square miles. Even today only 8 per cent of the land area is suitable for cultivation. Cliffs make up 27 per cent of it. Rock escarpments rise up sheer from the breakers. This is the domain of the sea fowl which from dawn to dusk wheel high overhead.

The original wooden dwellings were built among the hibiscus, the jasmine and the palms. An idyllic setting for a blood bath. . . .

THE END OF A DREAM?   It was a warm night with a north wind pulling the moon backwards through the wild, blanched clouds. The Pitcairn summer was at an end.

Fletcher Christian walked between the log-wood dwellings of the settlement his eight mutineers had constructed in so short a time. By his side was the statuesque Isabella, a shade short of his own height. They took pride in what they saw. There was a certain order that reminded Christian of England. And yet. . . .

Each day seemed to bring its own tensions. Christian well knew he could not hope to keep control of his eight feisty mutineers in this subtropical Shangri-la.

There was Edward Young. He was short of stature, of dark complexion, much like Susan, his artful, strong-willed Tahitian wife. Young was the most cultured of *Bounty*'s hard-core mutineers and quickly earned the respect of all the women.

There was John Williams and his Pashotu. Williams had been one of *Bounty*'s ratings. His propensity for violence was indicated by a scar on the back of his head by no means covered by his shock of black hair. Ashore he had proved co-operative. But there was an edginess, a tendency to jump too quickly in defence of his own interests.

And then Matthew Quintal, the youngest and lustiest of the mutineers who had come to Pitcairn. Heavily tattooed, and powerfully built, he seemed for the time to be mellowed in his unaccustomed domestic setting. But still there were occasional eruptions of the temperament which had gained him notoriety. Wooden walls were too fragile to keep out the sounds of his fights with Sarah. Would his propensity to lose control always be confined to his own cabin?

By now Christian, and others, were aware that 'Alexander Smith' was a pseudonym. 'Smith's' proper name was John Adams. No one asked him and he never volunteered the information why he had thought it necessary to enlist aboard the *Bounty* under a false name. What vile crimes had he committed in his dark, unchronicled past? From what had he been running away? His new wife Paurai did not seem to notice his face disfigured by smallpox and took pride in his well-made, heavily-tattooed body. She herself was suffering from an illness of throat and lungs. But there was no word of complaint.

William McKoy had been a brewery worker before enlisting as a rating aboard HMS *Bounty*. His hair and complexion were fair. But, stripped to the waist as he usually was, everyone had noticed the livid scar across his stomach, left-over of an unaccounted brawl from his pre-*Bounty* past. There was another scar across his throat. His wife Mary had had a baby daughter when he had taken her from Tahiti. Puzzled as to how to get her ashore at Pitcairn from the *Bounty* they had finally opened the end of a barrel, dropped the little girl inside and floated her ashore. For the sake of Mary and her child Christian hoped that violence was not a way of life with McKoy.

Isaac Martin, the tall American aged 30, was of sinewy build and, in the share-out of wives, had successfully insisted on taking John Adams's wife Jenny. No one had taken Jenny's feelings into account. Indeed, Christian may well have reflected, at no point had *anyone* considered the wants and wishes of these strong-willed, Polynesian beauties. When they tired of the novelty of their new situation was it possible that *they* might prove a force he would find difficult to contain?

Of the eight Pitcairn mutineers John Mills was the oldest. He had been 40 when he had enlisted on HMS *Bounty* two years before. He had accepted the Tahitian wife allotted to him without complaint; but then he spoke little. Everyone knew that the gunner's mate had hidden depths.

Finally there was William Brown the botanist. Were it not for the ugly scar across his face it might have been assumed that this nine-stone weakling was of passive disposition.

Fletcher Christian and Isabella had reached the edge of the encampment where the six islanders – four Tahitian, two Tubuaian – had erected their makeshift dwellings. Here was the most predictable source of trouble. Outside of the settlement the Englishmen had divided the 8 per cent of the island capable of cultivation into more or less equal shares. Among themselves, that is; they had allowed none for the Polynesians. Six men who had to share among them three women. . . . They bitterly resented being used by the Englishmen as if they had a right to their labour. Their women despised them and had a deep sense of alienation.

But Pitcairn afforded bread-fruit, yams and bananas aplenty, reflected Christian. And the men were cultivating their smallholdings with a will, making the best use of the plants which had remained aboard the *Bounty*.

But why, among all the islands of the Pacific, was *this* island uninhabited, reflected Christian? He had noticed strange petroglyphs scratched on the walls of caves. He had found the ruins of an ancient temple, a sun-bleached human skull resting on the central altar. Uninhabited now, it was clear that long before Captain Philip Cartaret made his famous entry regarding Pitcairn in 1767, Pitcairn had supported human life. What had caused it to die out or migrate?

Fletcher and Isabella had reached Ship Land Point beyond the curtain of banyan trees. They watched the angry breakers burst with incredible violence against the cliff face, drowning the beach where they had landed, and wondered what sort of future this tiny colony of ill-assorted human kind, lost to history, would bring upon itself. Then, peering through the spray to the left of Bounty Bay, they noticed a spurt of flame. Soon much of the bay area was lighted by flames leaping into the night sky. The *Bounty* was burning.

BIRTH AND DEATH.   By morning light *Bounty* had burned to the water line. Within another forty-eight hours of tempest their only link-line to the outside world need never have existed.

Some said Fletcher Christian had ordered her to be put to the torch as the final precaution against discovery.

Others had seen Quintal aboard her at nightfall, drunkenly rummaging for raw materials to complete his cabin. There was the story that he had accidentally upset a lamp.

Certain it is that not all the mutineers rejoiced at the loss of the *Bounty*. John Mills grieved. He had harboured the hope of a return to England. His daughter, who lived to be ninety-three, never tired of telling the tale of her father's tears at the destruction of the good ship *Bounty*.

In the months that followed, the resentment of the Polynesian men turned to hatred. Children were born, but they took no part in the celebrations.

The first child to be born on Pitcairn was Thursday October Christian, son of Fletcher and Isabella.

In time Fletcher Christian had three children; John Mills two; William McKoy three; Matthew Quintal five; Edward Young six; and John Adams four. But the background against which these English-Polynesian offspring were to be reared was one of intrigue and murder.

After surveying available land Christian had divided it into nine equal parts. There were nine white men, therefore there were nine plots. The six Polynesian men were left landless. Perhaps it was the scarcity of land that caused Christian to make this fatal miscalculation. Perhaps it was the assumption that the Polynesians would be content with their role as unpaid labourers. In the event, added to the scarcity of women among the Polynesians, it was to be a major factor in causing the blood bath that introduced hell into paradise.

But without the precipitate action of two of his

mutineers an uneasy peace might have been maintained for a limited period in Christian's dreamland.

In the first two years of the community's existence there were many births – and two deaths.

Pashotu, wife of John Williams, plunged to her death while gathering birds' eggs on a high cliff.

Paurai, wife of John Adams, died of the disease of the throat and lungs which she had brought with her from Tahiti.

Williams was the first to become morose and moody, resenting the domestic happiness of his fellow mutineers, and casting lustful glances at the three women shared among the Polynesian men.

Eventually Williams vocalized his demands. He wanted a wife. He went so far as to threaten to use the *Bounty* cutter to reach another island in search of women. In view of Pitcairn's isolation this was no more than a ploy, but Williams well knew that his fellow mutineers could not afford to take the risk of his absence. His skills as a blacksmith were of indispensable importance to them.

With or without the connivance of his fellow mutineers, Williams forced Nancy to leave Talaloo, and Adams forced Tinafanaea to leave the two Tubuaians.

Landless, exploited and, they felt, with little to lose, the Polynesians plotted revenge.

The most detailed account of the violent events of the years that followed 1792 is to be found in a book published in 1831 entitled *Narrative of a Voyage to the Pacific and the Bering Strait*. The account was written by Captain F. W. Beechey. He had called at Pitcairn in 1825 aboard HMS *Blossom*. He had read the fragmentary diary Edward Young had kept since their arrival on the island and had interviewed John Adams, by then revered as Pitcairn's patriarch. From these two sources Beechey provides a full account of the massacres.

MURDER IN PARADISE

THE FIRST WAVE. The bloodshed began when Nancy moved in with Williams. Her husband Talaloo, until now the only Polynesian not to have to share his wife, plotted murder. Expecting a move by John Adams to snatch one of the two wives remaining to be shared between the other five Polynesians, they followed Talaloo into the wilds of the island.

On a still day with a clothy weight to the sky that hid the sun, they resolved to murder the mutineers.

More astute than their husbands, the Polynesian women knew what to expect. Nancy in particular feared for her own life. Two or three of the others had mixed loyalties. But at this stage at least four of the Tahitian women had enough feeling for their men to want to warn them of what was to take place.

In sing-song voices within hearing of Fletcher Christian working in his garden they carried on a conversation.

'Why does black man sharpen axe?' one questioned.

'To kill white man', another responded.

Fletcher Christian stopped work. Isabella had taught him to respect the sharp cunning of the Tahitians. She'd given him an insight into their patterns of thought and reaction. They were quite capable of outwitting any Englishman – and outfighting him too, given the element of surprise.

He pondered the stage-managed conversation he had been intended to overhear. He asked no further question. Entering his cabin he took up his musket and filled it with powder only. It was not his intention to commit murder. It is likely that his sympathies lay with Talaloo rather than Jack Williams. But a plot was afoot. Its outcome must be prevented. To prevent carnage he must act on his own. To ask for help from the likes of Quintal or McKoy was to court a bloody outcome.

Alone, he went in search of the aggrieved Polynesians. Not far from the settlement he startled the Tubuaian Oho. Oho was alone. Poker-faced, Christian tackled him about the plot. What was going on? Where were the others?

Guilt distorted Oho's features. He stared sullenly at Christian. Then he spun on his heel and began to run to the trees.

To scare him into stopping, Christian discharged his musket.

Unaware that the musket had been purposely filled with powder only, Oho was convinced that Christian had tried to kill him. Running for his life he dodged through the trees, jumped the undergrowth, sped like a wild animal rejoining the pack.

He found Talaloo, the aggrieved husband. The two men ran together along the white-hot path through trees and rocks to the other side of the island. In the humid heat the occasional thicket of trees threw a moment of shade before they ran out into the glare again. The plot had been discovered. They had no firearms. They had no next move planned. Panic set in.

Word spread among the Polynesians. The plot was discovered. What were their options?

Irrationally, they concentrated their anger against Oho and Talaloo.

In the heavy heat of the evening they slunk back into the camp. Christian was still looking for them in the southern part of the island and was not in his cabin. They sought to ingratiate themselves with the Englishmen they knew to be of the most violent temperament. They met with stony faces and hard stares. Afraid, and in return for their skins, they promised to murder Oho and Talaloo.

Again they made for the southern part of the island where Christian was searching for them. They encountered Oho first and murdered him in cold blood. They failed to find Talaloo.

Talaloo edged back into the camp unnoticed after dark. Unnoticed, that is, except by his former wife Nancy, who was afraid that he would take her life.

She went to his cabin and expressed disdain for Williams, her new 'husband'. With fearful tears the consummate actress asked to be taken back. Talaloo was deceived. He trusted her sufficiently to permit her to prepare him a meal.

Nancy had planned it all. She had even prepared the poison. It was carefully stirred into Talaloo's stew-like meal. He died in agony within the hour.

One day; two murders.

CHRISTIAN'S CAVE.   In the weeks that followed there was much pretence. No one trusted anybody else. But the Polynesian men returned to the settlement and appeared to carry on as usual. Anger that would not quit seethed in their breasts.

Every day the sight of Nancy in company with Williams reminded them that John Adams was still without a mate. When would he make his move?

In these months of uneasy peace Fletcher Christian spent a great deal of time away from the settlement. Adams later recalled that he would leave the village for the high cliff overlooking the booming breakers. Here he had found himself a cave high in the rock face. The melancholy moods of former times had returned. For hours at a stretch, wordless, he would sit looking out over the vast expanse of ocean. The women fancied that he was looking towards England. Brooding over the strange fate that had brought him to this isolated spot on the globe. They imagined that he was fretting for home and family. Rehearsing in his mind the events that had made him lead a mutiny. Reviewing the events which had caused his break with Bligh. Sorrowing for the sceptred isle to which he could never return.

This was all fancy, conjecture. But given the temperament of Fletcher Christian we can be almost certain that the thoughts that preoccupied his mind found their common denominator in guilt for actions past.

Almost certainly he was taking responsibility for the death of Bligh and the loyal men he had last seen in

Bounty's launch. Reproaching himself for the capture of the Englishmen on Tahiti and for the fate he felt he knew had been theirs.

BLIGH'S RETURN. Bligh had arrived back in England on 14 March 1790.

His arrival was not front-page news. The preoccupation of the time was with a revolution in France which threatened to unsettle the throne of England.

But in Admiralty circles William Bligh was hailed as a hero. His backers were soon planning a second bread-fruit voyage for him. A court martial in October to enquire into the seizure of HMS *Bounty* honourably acquitted Bligh of responsibility for her loss.

The government ordered the Admiralty to send out an armed vessel to apprehend the mutineers. The vessel was the twenty-four gun frigate, *Pandora*.

As Christian had anticipated, Tahiti was the first recourse for those sent in search of the mutineers. The *Pandora* arrived at Tahiti on 23 March 1791. Fourteen of the sixteen crew members who had remained on Tahiti were either captured or surrendered. All were confined in irons to a 'round house' built on *Pandora*'s quarter deck – eleven feet by eighteen.

The other mutineers were dead. One had been killed by his fellow countrymen, and the other by islanders.

Pandora sailed from Tahiti on 8 May and spent some time searching unsuccessfully for Christian and his crew. Their search was extensive, but did not take in Pitcairn.

On 28 August *Pandora* was wrecked off the Great Barrier Reef. Of the crew of 120, thirty-one were drowned. Of the fourteen prisoners, four were drowned.

Four of the ship's boats were used to sail to Timor whence the remaining prisoners were taken to England for trial. The courts martial began at Portsmouth on 18 September 1791. Those put on trial were Joseph Coleman, Charles Norman, Thomas McIntosh, Peter Heywood, James Morrison, John Millward, William Muspratt, Thomas Burkett, Thomas Ellison and Michael Byrne.

Coleman, Norman, McIntosh and Byrne were acquitted. As for Heywood, Morrison, Muspratt, Millward, Burkett and Ellison they were found guilty and sentenced to death.

In the event, three of them were pardoned. Heywood and Morrison were pardoned on a technicality. Muspratt was pardoned after twelve judges had weighed the testimony of each mutineer and taken into account the fact that Muspratt had requested that Norman should be acquitted as blameless.

On 29 October 1792 aboard HMS *Brunswick*, Millward, Burkett and Ellison were hanged.

THE SECOND WAVE. The Polynesians had been expecting John Adams to take one of their women long before he did so. He chose Tinafanaea who had been shared by the two Tubuaians.

Wretched desperation possessed the Polynesians. They had nothing to lose. No land or status in this island white men had made their own. Only the chains of exploitation; and the almost daily brutal mistreatment at the hands of insensitive louts like McKoy and Quintal.

They would murder the Englishmen.

The plot was carefully hatched, out of earshot of both the women and the mutineers. And the day carefully chosen.

It dawned humid with light cloud.

They watched the women and children set off for the far side of the island.

They saw Edward Young climb until he was out of sight (and sound) of the settlement. High on the far side of the cliff he was taking his turn keeping watch for passing ships. He would be absent all day.

Isaac Martin suspected nothing when Tetaheite asked to borrow musket and ammunition to shoot hogs. Minutes later he heard a shot being fired. He assumed a hog had been bagged. In fact Jack Williams had been shot dead at point blank range. Williams had stolen the wife of Talaloo and was the first focus for their hatred.

By now Timoa and Nehow had also acquired firearms. Manalee's part in the plot was to remain in the settlement so that suspicions would not be aroused. If things went badly wrong he had undertaken to raise the alarm.

But there was a last-minute change of plan.

With one mutineer dead and all the Polynesians armed, it was decided that they had best remain together. Manalee was working with Mills and McKoy. The other Polynesians approached and asked them for permission for Manalee to join them to help bring back the hog. Permission was granted.

Four polynesians, three of them armed, made directly for the home of Fletcher Christian.

The aloof, melancholy, well-educated young man who had led the mutiny still inspired respect among both Polynesians and mutineers. But among the Polynesians he also inspired fear. If anyone could put an end to their doings it was him.

They found him working in his garden. He turned to face his assassins. He realized their purpose too late. Suddenly his heart turned to ice and his bowels to water. They fired. Fletcher Christian fell mortally wounded. Through the white, cold sweat of pain he thought he saw the destruction of his entire enterprise. Within minutes he was dead.

Years later when the story reached home, the myth-makers found this aspect of the tale most difficult to accept. How could the life of the hero of the story be ended so suddenly and so pointlessly? Their wishful thinking was the origin of the belief that Christian escaped the carnage, sailed the seas on some makeshift boat to his native Cumbria and was the original Ancient Mariner of Coleridge's poem. The connection of Coleridge with Wordsworth and the friendship of the Wordsworths with the Christians seemed to lend credence to the myth. But myth it unquestionably was. Among the most definite finds of Glynn Christian's months on Pitcairn was the place of his great ancestor's violent death.

McKoy, who had always thought of the Polynesians as 'the enemy' and treated them with suspicion, rumbled their plot first. He jumped to the correct conclusion when he discovered that three of them were armed. In a frenzy of panic he tried to warn the others. He found Mills stubborn. He was arguing with him when Tetaheite approached. Mills, who had always enjoyed a good relationship with the Polynesians, refused to accept the upshot of what he regarded as McKoy's suspicious imagination. For a moment even McKoy was off guard. When Tetaheite told him that two Polynesians were rummaging among his things, he failed to see through the ruse. He set off for home at a fast gallop. Tetaheite had succeeded in separating the two Englishmen. The plotters emerged from their cover and shot Mills where he stood.

Hearing another shot, McKoy knew that he had been fooled. He had no difficulty persuading Quintal to join him. They ran towards Christian's home and saw his corpse sprawled in the garden before they reached it. McKoy and Quintal, thoroughly shaken, ran into the forested slopes of the nearby hills.

From their place of concealment they heard two more shots. Isaac Martin the American and Brown the botanist had now been murdered.

Unexpectedly, some of the women had returned from the far side of the island. Sarah Quintal was quick to realize what was afoot. Finding John Adams working in his garden she told him to take to the hills or suffer the fate of his confederates. John Adams joined McKoy and Quintal.

Amazed at their own success, the Polynesians began to take over their former masters' homes. However, knowing that Edward Young could be expected to return in early evening from his hilltop eyrie they remained on the alert. But it was Adams they sighted first. They saw him in the shadows emerge from the bush and dart towards his home. He had come to collect supplies. Instantly an attempt was made to murder him. But the musket mis-

Bounty Bay where the mutineers and their women put ashore.

The rock face where Fletcher Christian, and later John Adams, withdrew for solitude.

Considering the bloody nature of the island's settlement it is significant that life for the islanders today centres around their little church.

Pitcairn's only store has to try and meet all the shopping needs of the islanders. The increasing rarity of visitors make them especially welcome.

fired. A second shot was fired. When the smoke cleared Adams was badly wounded but by no means dead. He surrendered and asked for mercy. The bleeding man was dragged towards Feltcher Christian's home – past Christian's dead body. When Edward Young returned to camp he was captured and taken to join Adams.

As the remaining women and children, innocent of what had taken place, began to return to the settlement raindrops like pinpricks touched their faces. Cumulus clouds, earlier in the day as innocuous as flowers afloat on a pond, had begun to boil, their edges brilliant as marble against the blackening air. As the women scurried for the cover of their homes they were entirely unprepared for the fact that they were now in the hands of the Polynesians, fierce with macabre triumph.

Through that inclement night and many more that followed, McKoy and Quintal remained in hiding in the mountainous region of the island.

Among the four Polynesians everyone was giving the orders. Soon there was serious conflict over the available women. Manalee, after a bloody fight with another man, bolted for the tree-covered hills where McKoy and Quintal still held out. After some time he found them. He was treated with hostility and suspicion. When Adams was sufficiently recovered he was dispatched by the Polynesians from the home of Fletcher Christian with a message to McKoy and Quintal. The substance of it would appear to have been that if they murdered Manalee they would be permitted to rejoin the community. They wasted no time in committing the murder.

It was now the turn of the women to take a hand in the murders. The widows of the murdered men entered into a plan with Edward Young to kill the remaining Polynesians. Young shot Nehow and the women took care of the rest. Of the fifteen men who had landed on Pitcairn from the *Bounty* in 1790, eleven had been murdered. There were now four men on the island and eleven women. The date was 3 October 1793.

Of the nine Pitcairn mutineers, five outlived by eleven

months those of their former companions who were brought to British justice and hanged aboard HMS *Brunswick*. McKoy, Quintal, Adams and Young would survive a little longer.

THE LAST ENGLISHMAN.   The blood bath did not bring peace to the island.

Before it, the women, a scarce commodity, had been relatively well treated. After it they were re-allocated, two or three to a man. No longer a cherished commodity, they began to be ill treated. Quintal and McKoy, violent by temperament, took ill treatment to the last refinement of excess. When Sarah Quintal returned home from egg-hunting with little to show for her precarious efforts, her husband (literally) bit off her ear!

Even Edward Young, usually noted for his deference towards women and his civilized behaviour, would appear to have lapsed during this period.

As a result, *all* the women deserted their men. They huddled together in one cabin protecting their off-spring.

In this ridiculous cold-war situation no one was prepared to make the first move. Eventually Young decided that it was down to him.

He walked over to the women's hut and was horrified by what he saw. Jenny, formerly the wife of Isaac Martin, was playing with a human skull. He expressed his horror. Jenny triumphantly replied that it was the skull of Jack Williams!

Upon enquiry Young discovered (in the words quoted from his journal) that the women had in their possession 'the heads of the five white men'. Young's journal, no longer extant, fell into the hands of Captain Beechey in 1825. He accepted the reference to 'five white men' as firm indication that Fletcher Christian had died on Pitcairn. There is no reason to doubt his conclusion.

But on that scorching, oily, South Seas summer day in 1794 Edward Young was sickened. His temper rose. In extravagant language he accused the women of being

66

'savages' and demanded that they bury the bones of the dead men.

The incident closed with Young making an undignified retreat in the face of eleven very angry women.

However, when, a few weeks later, Jenny announced their intention of constructing a boat in which to sail away, the men, after a brief discussion among themselves, offered their assistance.

The project never had a chance of success and, even if it had, the 'assistance' rendered by the men made sure that the chances were dashed. On the day the boat was launched in Bounty Bay it sank within yards of the shore and, bedraggled and sullen, the women waded back to the beach. The only positive result of this farcical enterprise was that the women agreed to bury the bones of the murdered victims (ten months after death!).

The unhappiness of the women deepened as the months went by. Their desperation showed in their eyes. A number of them were already guilty of murder, and the men well knew that, given the opportunity, they would not hesitate to commit murder again. The men concealed muskets in order to defend themselves and uncovered 'conspiracies' of one sort or another every two or three weeks.

On 13 November 1794 the women actually attacked. But they were not united. While some of them had a fixed determination to rid the island of men, a few still had a degree of attachment to the men they had once regarded as their 'husbands'. Edward Young, in particular, seemed to inspire respect among the women.

An uneasy truce prevailed between the sexes during the summer of 1794-95. From time to time groups of women went off and hid themselves in unfrequented parts of the island. Things seemed to improve for a time when, after months of hard work, the men succeeded in building two canoes. For a while their hauls of fish improved. They traded the fish with the women in return for meat and yams.

As crops began to grow successfully it even seemed at

one time that the women might come to accept their lot.

But Bill McKoy and Matt Quintal put a stop to any thoughts of domestic harmony, or even peaceful co-existence, by their behaviour following a discovery on 20 April 1797.

On that day, after a period of experimentation with the roots of trees and sugar cane, they succeeded in distilling spirits. The discovery was made by McKoy. Quintal made his contribution by converting the *Bounty*'s kettles into a still. Bouts of wild intoxication, in which many of the women participated, followed. Under the influence of alcohol McKoy jumped from a high cliff to his death.

But it was Sarah Quintal's death, in similar circumstances, which led to an eruption of further conflicts. Matt Quintal announced that he was entitled to another wife and that he would settle for none other than 'Mainmast', Fletcher Christian's widow.

Edward Young took violent exception to this.

Quintal, more or less permanently intoxicated, announced that if he couldn't have Mainmast he would butcher the Christian children.

Adams and Young decided on a pre-emptive strike. With an axe. Quintal died instantly.

There were now twenty children on the island. Sully, aged 10, had come with her mother on board the *Bounty*. In addition there were Fletcher Christian's three children – Thursday October, 9, Charles, 8, and Mary, 6. There were three 7-year-olds: Matthew Quintal the second, Daniel McKoy and Elizabeth Mills. John Mills was 6. The remaining children were infants born between 1794 and 1799. With the nine remaining women and two remaining men, Edward Young and John Adams, the population of Pitcairn had reached thirty-one.

When Edward Young died from consumption (TB) in 1800, John Adams was left the unlikely patriarch of this strange island community.

DISCOVERY AND CHANGE

THE 'BOUNTY' BIBLE. No one knew it, but the murder and mayhem which had thus far dogged the island community were all in the past.

The Pitcairn colony was about to be transformed beyond recognition.

The transformation began with a discovery.

The discovery was made by Adams and Young among the possessions of Fletcher Christian's widow. It was made about twelve months before Young's death.

The item discovered came to be know as 'The *Bounty* Bible'.

Its discovery brought back a distant recollection to the memories of Young and Adams. Once, while Fletcher Christian was alive, an attempt had been made to organize a church service. Immobile and dying from consumption, Edward Young had much time for reflection. What chance did this tiny group of souls perched on an isolated rock in the South Pacific have in the future? He had certain advantages which he had failed to pass on to his fellow islanders. Among these were a sound education and a Christian upbringing.

The final months of Young's life were spent teaching John Adams to read, with the Bible as his only textbook. Adams proved an apt pupil. Soon he had assimilated not only the rudiments of literacy but the principles upon the basis of which his textbook had been written.

Soon John Adams, his skin harshly red and pock-marked, had introduced morning and evening worship services, plus two formal services on Sundays.

Women and children alike noticed a change in his character and outlook. Adams had not just encountered the Book, but the Man in the Book. And that had made a drastic difference.

Conscious that death was approaching, Edward Young,

in a thin voice like a trickle squeezed through rust, indicated to those around him that the island was now in good hands. They all had a past to live down. He and Adams had collaborated in a murder. Others had been responsible for the shedding of blood. They, all of them, had a past that had to be dealt with. But there was a way. . . .

THE WAY. The last Englishman, the only surviving *Bounty* mutineer on Pitcairn, with his mysterious record before the bread-fruit expedition, and his reputation for violence, drunkenness, promiscuity – and even murder, had embraced the religion of Jesus Christ. Unquestionably the conversion of Adams saved the little community from destruction. At 36 he had experienced a new birth – and he never looked back.

Part of his conversion involved coming to terms with his past. It was at this time that he abandoned the name Alexander Smith (assumed when he had enlisted on the *Bounty*) and reverted to his proper name, John Adams. As he presided over the daily worship services, and the two services on Sunday, the women and children learned not only about the stories from Scripture which so fascinated Adams but they received brief glimpses into his changed character.

It was, evidently, possible to grow up in mid-eighteenth-century England and receive as little instruction in the precepts of Christianity as one who had grown up in Tahiti. Adams's fascination with the Bible was completely fresh; the stories came to him brand new. Daily he riveted the attention of the children with his vivid retelling of what he himself had so recently learned. Jesus Christ, until now no more than an expletive to be used when he had run out of four-letter words, became a real, living presence in the life of Adams. Years later the children now gathered around his knee would testify to his transformation and recall some of the glimpses he allowed them to have into his life. The details of his sordid past were never spoken of. Except, that is, in generalizations:

70

he was, he said, a death-deserving sinner but Jesus Christ had died the death he deserved and his sins were lost in the fathomless depths of God's forgetfulness.

Adams spoke of a peace that passed all understanding, a joy that no man could take from him, and a sense of meaning and purpose newly acquired. It would appear that he hardly needed to have done so. All were apparent in his life.

John Adams carried with him a deep sense of his responsibility for the present and future generations on the island. He often withdrew to what had become known as 'Christian's cave' high on the cliff face. There he would read, meditate and pray to a God who was as real to him as if he were his constant companion. On one occasion in the cave he professed to have had some kind of 'vision' or 'mystical experience'.

His Christianity became contagious. The children caught it and practised it with enthusiasm. H. M. S. Richards says it this way: 'The children became quiet, peaceful and hard-working. They behaved as one family, united in love under the fatherly hold of John Adams.' They even erected their own classroom in order to formalize the instruction that Adams daily gave them.

The women emerged out of a past in which, in order to survive, they had been guilty of all manner of crime and indecency. One by one their hearts were softened. Exposed to the *Bounty* Bible and the Christ who lived through the life of John Adams they too began a process of change.

A NEW GENERATION. Beginning with 1806 a new generation began to be born on Pitcairn. Thursday October Christian married Susan, the widow of Edward Young. Charles Christian married Sully. There were other weddings.

The ceremonies were conducted by John Adams who used a prayer book (like the Bible, once the property of Fletcher Christian) and a ring that had belonged to one of the midshipmen.

71

Into the little community, now free of the old tensions but still preoccupied with the struggle to survive from day to day, more children were born. In 1809 Mayhew Folger, an American captain, discovered the island of the mutineers for the first time. On many occasions between the landing on Pitcairn and the death of Edward Young ships had come near the island, the look-out had given the signal and all fires had been extinguished and movement stopped until the danger had passed. This procedure was not followed after Adams's conversion. Hence the discovery of the Pitcairn community by the American captain and, with that discovery, the beginning of the legend that spread throughout the English-speaking world and beyond. The legend of an idyllic community centred around a rugged-faced patriarch, clamorous with children, but involved in a day-to-day fight for economic survival. The legend took root in the popular imagination of the Western World – and has remained there ever since.

The island soon attracted more callers. British and American vessels dropped anchor off shore. Longboats manned by the new generation of Pitcairners went out to greet the passengers and crews. Everywhere Pitcairn was known for the high standard of morality instilled by John Adams from the precepts discovered in the *Bounty* Bible. Royal Navy officers, no longer interested in the fact that a mutiny was part of the story, reported on this island of well-built, sunburnt men and beautiful, nut-brown women. Tales were told of the simple manner of life and the Puritan values of the island. The new generation had resolutely turned its back on the excesses which had characterized island behaviour before the *Bounty* Bible wrought its miracle.

On 29 March 1829, at the age of 65, John Adams died expressing an assurance of everlasting salvation. In a ceremony that would have done justice to the English obsession with pomp and pageantry, he was laid to rest in a grave at the foot of the great cliff, not far from the cave in which he had spent so much time over the years and, by his own testimony, had once seen an angel in a dream.

THE COMING OF STRANGERS.   With the death of the patriarch it would have been better, all things considered, if his place had been taken by one of Fletcher Christian's fine sons. But in the last decade of his life Adams had been conscious of the need of the islanders for an education of the sort which he could not provide. Thus it was that, on his death, his place was taken by strangers. Men who were not part of the island's story and saw the dominant position which they could create for themselves on this Puritan island as a means to exploit the little community. Above all, the strangers had had no part in the conversion which had so transformed the lives of the islanders in the early years of the century.

The first of these strangers to influence the life of the island was John Buffett. Buffett was a young man with fierce eyes, tempestuous good humour and an artisan's education. By the time the whaler *Cyrus* anchored off Pitcairn in October 1823 he had already had a life of adventure and been exposed to most of the experiences a man might encounter in a lifetime at sea.

Buffett came ashore as a result of an appeal by John Adams to his captain. Was it possible, Adams had asked, that anyone was aboard the *Cyrus* who could take over from him the function of educator to the islanders? Buffett was put ashore. As he struggled up the cliff to the settlement, his moon-thrown shadow walking behind him, no one noticed that someone else had jumped ship and come ashore.

Not until the *Cyrus* was well away from Pitcairn did 19-year-old John Evans emerge from his hiding.

Soon Buffett and Evans were gaping wide-eyed at the beautiful chestnut-cheeked girls on the island. Adams soon made sure that they understood the score. It was marriage or nothing. In no time Dorothy Young was asking for his permission to marry Buffett, and his own daughter Rachael his permission to marry Evans. With many misgivings he conducted the ceremonies.

Buffett established himself as schoolmaster, and for two years things seemed to go well. But soon he was looking around for other 'available' women. When his affair with one of the late Matt Quintal's daughters came to light he lost his standing on the island. In order to remain he had to make certain undertakings. In the event it was his paramour who, rather than face the Puritan reaction of the island, left for other shores.

Two more strangers arrived in October 1828. They were George Nobbs, an Englishman, and Noah Bunker, an American. Both men had been attracted by the legend of the island which had caught hold in their respective countries. Nobbs was an educated man and able to take over from the disgraced Buffett. Unquestionably the best of the bunch of strangers who settled on the island, Nobbs lost no time in winning and marrying Sarah Christian, granddaughter of Fletcher. Hence it was Nobbs upon whom the mantle of John Adams fell on his death in March 1829.

Nobbs was forced to seek a solution to a problem that John Adams had never been able to face. The problem: insufficient natural resources in terms of spring water and food to support an island population which now exceeded eighty.

Within months of Adams's death the problem had grown to urgent proportions. Everyone understood it. But not everyone was enthusiastic about the solution proposed by Nobbs. Having been in contact with one of the chiefs on Tahiti, Nobbs proposed that the islanders leave the isolated rock in the South Pacific which had been their home since the mutineers and their consorts landed, and accept the gift of a tract of land on Tahiti, the island from which the women had originally come.

The sailing took place on 7 March 1831 on the *Lucy Anne*. Almost all wept copiously. But the sadness of the women who had accompanied the mutineers to Pitcairn forty-one years before was mixed with a feeling of excitement. They were going to see the relations they had never thought to see again.

74

The landing at Tahiti was almost as emotional as the farewell from Pitcairn. The women embraced brothers and sisters now grown old as they had.

But the experiment was not to be successful. The revolutionary change which had been brought about in the lives of the Pitcairners in the years following the discovery of the *Bounty* Bible made them a race apart from the promiscuous Tahitians. The long years of separation had also rendered them vulnerable to certain diseases, some of them killers, rampant on Tahiti.

Within days of their landing no fewer than fourteen of their number, including Thursday October Christian, elder son of Fletcher Christian, had died from what they termed 'the plague'.

By comparison with these tragedies the privations of Pitcairn seemed unimportant. There spread a growing feeling that a great mistake had been made; that a drastic decision had been taken upon which God's opinion had not been sought.

When a schooner put in at Tahiti less than six weeks after they had landed, a considerable group of Pitcairners, including most of the Christian family, took the opportunity to return to their island home.

Within six months the entire surviving population of Pitcairn had returned to their isolated paradise.

IN THE GRIP OF A MADMAN. No sooner had they adjusted to life on Pitcairn again than they had to live through another nightmare.

A passing freighter put ashore a 70-year-old man. His name was Joshua Hill. He claimed to have orders from His Majesty King William IV of England to assume the government of the island. Behind an impressive face was the mind of a madman.

Hill was a religious maniac with a taste for power. He carried no mandate from the British government.

He introduced a draconian system of 'sin sanctions' which might have made John Adams turn in his grave. He gained the sympathy of many of the islanders, including all of the women, when he turned the sanctions upon the men who had brought the drinking habit, long dead on Pitcairn, back from Tahiti.

Soon his regime followed one excess upon another. Someone mentioned Buffett's affair, now almost a decade in the past. Hill ordered that Buffett should be flogged for his sins of the flesh.

On a day when birds sang and the grass steamed warmly he had Buffett lashed to a tree. One of the Quintals was detailed to inflict the flogging. The time came, the islanders had gathered. Quintal's hand was raised to lay on the lash.

A tall, impressive man stepped forward. It was Charles Christian, the oldest man on the island and the second son of Fletcher Christian.

Charles Christian grasped Quintal by the wrist and took the whip from him. No words were spoken, but Hill went into a paroxysm of hysterical anger.

Christian looked down at the antics of the freakish old man.

Hill had lost face. He decided to have the punishment carried out under cover of darkness. At this stage he had enough friends to make this possible. One night John Buffett received his flogging in the sacred confines of Pitcairn's church.

He branded the three strangers – Nobbs, Buffett and Evans (Bunker was by now dead) – as the enemy within. Certainly they represented one of the chief barriers between himself and absolute power. He encouraged their wives to leave them, pouring all manner of imprecations upon their heads. Eventually he succeeded in driving them from the island.

The Pitcairners did not unite against Joshua Hill until Quintal's 8-year-old daughter, caught in the act of stealing yams, was sentenced to death.

The dictator had made a bad move. Quintal had been one of his staunchest supporters. But Quintal had enough of his father about him to refuse to be governed by a tyrant when it was against his interests.

He defied Hill to his face. Hill tackled him with a sword and told him to confess his sins for he was about to die.

Quintal acted swiftly. He grabbed the old man by the shoulders. Spun him round. Disarmed him. Hill was left standing, a figure of ridicule.

He never recovered his power again.

By now Nobbs, Buffett and Evans had reached islands from which it was possible to send letters to the British government. Vehemently they protested that the island should be put under the government of such a maniac.

The delayed reaction of the British government came in 1841. They sent Captain Elliott to place the island 'under the protection of the English flag'. Elliott remained long enough to ensure the establishment of a primitive system of law and constitutional practice.

Queen Victoria, who had by now acceded in London, hearing of the trying times through which the Pitcairners had recently lived, sent them gifts, including an organ for the church. For the remainder of her long reign she took a detailed interest in the life of the island. Perhaps she felt that, in its Puritan ways, it reflected her own outlook on life.

Victoria's distant matriarchy replaced that of Isabella Christian, Mainmast. The widow of the long-dead leader of the *Bounty* mutineers, whose memory stretched back to the visits of Captain Cook to her island home of Tahiti, died in 1841.

CRISIS AND CONSOLIDATION

THE EVACUATION.   The problems that George Nobbs had sought to address by the evacuation to Tahiti in 1831 became more acute with every passing year.

But with a consciousness of the problem, there also existed among the islanders horrific memories of the weeks away from what they had come to see as their God-appointed home. Vivid tales were told on summer evenings around communal fires under the racing sky. 'Just landed, and fourteen dead, including Thursday October Christian.' The old women talked with faint, whispering sadness, heads on one side, of the greatness of other times.

But it was no time for reminiscing when the island men met in the Pitcairn church to make a final decision on one of the long South Sea summer evenings before Christmas 1855.

The island's population stood at 187. The island's resources simply could not support them.

After a heated debate the decision was taken to evacuate. Lord Palmerston's government in London had offered them Norfolk Island.

This time the evacuation was organized carefully. On 2 May 1856 all 187 men, women and children were packed on board HMS *Morayshire* with as many of their possessions and as much of their livestock as could be wedged in. Eyes glittered like broken glass, but the misgivings that most had were smothered by the assurances of the British government that Norfolk Island, not far from New Zealand, was ideally suited to their purpose and would sustain their population for the foreseeable future.

It is not clear whether they were told that, until the recent past, Norfolk Island had been Britain's 'devil's island', a penal colony reserved for those transported for the very worst offences. Most Pitcairners hated it on sight.

It had nothing to match the lush ruggedness of the little island they persisted in seeing as home. The buildings that remained spoke eloquently of the manner of life of the prisoners who had, relatively recently, vacated the island. The only buildings there were those connected with the administration of a penal colony.

Those who had said, 'Don't go!' felt themselves vindicated. On 2 December 1858 a number of families bearing the names of Young and McKoy sought passage on board the *Mary Ann* to return to Pitcairn. In the months and years that followed, others returned, among them all the descendants of Thursday October Christian. Others remained on Norfolk Island, organized an efficient economy and grew to regard it as home. Among them were all the descendants of Charles Christian. Hence those who counted the great *Bounty* mutineer among their ancestors became divided between the two island communities.

NEW LIFE ON PITCAIRN.   The first families to return to Pitcairn were in for a shock. They arrived at dawn. As they reached the settlement a sea mist came up from the bay and wrapped them round until damp rolled off their eyebrows.

When the mist was burned off by the sun they realized what they had suspected was true. Someone had lived in Adamstown in their absence. There were signs of fires all over the place. Above all, their wooden homes had very largely been dismantled.

After two days of living rough they discovered a clue that would solve the mystery. In the school building – largely intact – they found a message on one of the slates. It was from Captain J. N. Knowles. On a voyage from San Francisco his ship had been wrecked seventy miles south-west of Pitcairn. He had brought off his crew on a deserted island then left thirty of them there and, with six of his crew, set off in the ship's boat to find help. After many days the great breakers had flung their boat with them in it ashore at the foot of the great cliff that fronted

Bounty Bay (after the fashion of the mutineers' arrival so many years before). Their boat had been completely destroyed in the pounding surf.

Pitcairn had not been what they were looking for, but at least it provided some temporary shelter and plenty of food. In the months that they had spent on the island they had used the timber from the Adamstown cabins to construct a boat which would take them on from Pitcairn. Aware of Pitcairn's story and embarrassed by their desecration of so important a piece of history as Adamstown, they named the boat they had built out of its timbers, the *John Adams*.

Adamstown was rebuilt.

Fourteen years later Captain Knowles revisited the island, introduced himself to its inhabitants and immediately struck up a rapport with them.

Knowles's contact with the island was to be an historic one. On his third visit, in 1876, he brought with him letters and religious papers from San Francisco. These came from James White and John Loughborough, among the leaders of a rapidly growing religious movement in the United States: the Seventh-day Adventist Church.

Three-quarters of a century had elapsed since the *Bounty* Bible conversion of Pitcairn. During his lifetime John Adams had sent to England for a Church of England missionary. None had come to so isolated a spot.

In the years that followed Adams's death – years in which the Puritan heritage of the island was maintained with some difficulty by a handful of prominent personalities – other requests were sent to England for a clergyman. Given that Pitcairn was something of a living legend, it is somewhat surprising that none ever came. The contact in 1876 with the Seventh-day Adventists was the first contact of the Pitcairn community with an organized Church.

Captain Knowles was able to speak well of the Adventists. Perhaps he saw similarities between what he knew of the Adventist life-style in the United States and what he knew was best in the Pitcairn tradition.

One source of revenue for Pitcairn is postage stamps. The island's story from the mutiny on the 'Bounty' to the bicentenary is told in stamps. The island's flaura and fauna, the fish and cereal crops so essential to her economy, are all on the stamps. On every stamp: the Queen's head. Pitcairn claims to be the most patriotic of all British countries. Every home has at least one portrait of the Queen.

Method of Bounty's
Transportation of the
Young Bread-fruit
Plants in Pots.

PITCAIRN ISLANDS 5c

PITCAIRN ISLANDS $1

THE ISLAND CHURCH

PITCAIRN ISLANDS 35c

POLISTES TADIUSAE DALLA TORRE

PITCAIRN ISLANDS 4c

SOUTH PACIFIC COMMISSION 1947/1972

Pitcairn Islands

4c

H.M. ARMED VESSEL BOUNTY

PITCAIRN ISLANDS

1D

PANTALA FLAVESCENS

DEVIL'S NEEDLE

PITCAIRN ISLANDS 15c

MOTHS

PITCAIRN ISLANDS 10c

5c

Pitcairn Islands

Pitcairn Islands 15c

'Elwyn's Trousers'

CLEANING WAHOO

PITCAIRN
ISLANDS 9c

PITCAIRN ISLANDS 5c

'Auntie-and-Ann'

The leader of the island community, another Thursday October Christian, read the letters from White and Loughborough very carefully and studied the trunkful of literature they had sent. Every family became involved in earnest discussion.

There was much in Seventh-day Adventist teaching that caused them to rejoice. Somehow, in the Puritan tradition passed down through the generations on the island, had come the belief that salvation was something that had to be *deserved, worked at, earned*. The Adventist teaching of Righteousness by Faith in Jesus Christ alone brought a sense of tremendous liberation to men and women who knew, in their heart of hearts, that they could never deserve salvation, and that sin was a day-to-day reality regardless of how hard they tried. From the writings of Loughborough and White they discovered that salvation came through repentance and self-surrender; that by his faultless life and blameless death Jesus Christ had won salvation for them. The detailed study of Paul's letters half a century before, had led John Adams to catch a glimmering of this Gospel, but it had never taken root. It had seemed more natural to him that you had to paddle your own canoe to the Kingdom of God.

They discovered that they were 'saved', assured of heaven and eternal life, at the point when they came to Jesus Christ. And that, having been saved, their lives were revolutionized from the inside by *his* power. By accepting the sacrifice of Christ on their behalf, argued James White (quoting the letter to the Hebrews, chapter four), they 'entered into rest', the rest from their efforts to deserve what they could never deserve, to earn what was beyond their power to earn. They learned too that this rest was symbolized by the seventh-day Sabbath (Saturday), a day to be kept sacred, not in order to be saved but because they were saved. A symbol of rest and an indication that they had 'entered into rest'.

The Pitcairners rejoiced in this liberating Gospel, but choked on some of the peripheral aspects of Seventh-day Adventist teaching. The Adventist emphasis on health and temperance made sense to them. But the Adventist dietary taboos – including the eating of pig meat, the island's delicacy – seemed to them impracticable. They found the taboo to be grounded in Scripture, and suspected that it was based on sound, scientific principles. But what was all right in the far-off land of 'America' – a fabulous land, if you were to listen to Captain Knowles – might not work out so well in the South Seas.

Study continued, and a revival began. But no decision was taken with regard to affiliation with the Seventh-day Adventist Church.

Not, that is, until ten years hence. In October 1886 John Tay arrived on Pitcairn from Oakland, California, the first missionary to Pitcairn, and a Seventh-day Adventist. Thursday October Christian II, who had been studying the trunkful of literature from San Francisco for a decade, welcomed Tay and opened discussions with him right away. Christian and Simon Young, who had been appointed leader of the Pitcairn church largely because of his grasp of Adventist teaching, had long discussions with Tay which lasted well into the night. The islanders approved Tay's request to remain until the arrival of the next ship.

In the weeks that followed, evenings were spent with Tay either preaching in the church or conducting Bible studies in the home of Simon Young. When, five weeks later, the next ship hove into view, every Pitcairn Islander had embraced the Seventh-day Adventist faith.

Tay returned to California with the news. Excited at being part of the *Bounty* legend, the Seventh-day Adventist Church commissioned the building of a mission ship for use in the South Seas. On completion it was named the *Pitcairn*. And Pitcairn was its first port of call.

It arrived in 1890. And 1890 was Pitcairn's centenary year. One hundred years after the arrival of the mutineers and their Polynesian 'wives', the entire Pitcairn community were baptized by immersion. Baptism by immersion was another Adventist practice, symbolizing identification with the death, burial and resurrection of Jesus Christ.

Three Adventist couples had been on board the *Pitcairn*, among them Mr. and Mrs. John Tay.

A century on from that mass baptism the inhabitants of Pitcairn Island continue to be Seventh-day Adventists.

Ian Ball, who wrote *Pitcairn: Children of the Bounty* after a visit to the island with a television crew, was at pains to explain the Adventist connection on Pitcairn: 'The attraction Seventh-day Adventism held for the little colony had . . . a threefold explanation.

'First, and the most significant, the islanders were flattered by the attention paid to their little flock by urbane and scholarly men from California and the east coast of America. . . .

'Second, Adventism held out for the islanders a heightened form of spiritual excitement in its root belief that the Second Coming of Christ, a visible return of the Saviour, was near at hand. . . .

'And third, Adventism held out a special attraction to the women of the community. With its religious, rather than purely social or legal, prohibition against the use of alcohol and stimulants in general, it offered the women a unique way of keeping their menfolk under more orderly control.'

Ask the Pitcairners, and they concede that there is much truth in Ball's observations. But to his three points they add a fourth which they point out is the most basic of all: through Seventh-day Adventism they had discovered 'the freedom of the Gospel'.

EPILOGUE: PITCAIRN TODAY

BICENTENARY OF THE BOUNTY COLONY. What do modern visitors make of Pitcairn?

Surprisingly, the picture they paint is as idyllic, in one sense, as that painted by Captain Mayhew Folger – who 'rediscovered' the island in 1809 – and the other seafarers who came calling in the years thereafter.

A scientific study has been done by a team of German doctors. They reported their findings in the medical journal *Physis* (8 August 1985). After a long stay on this most hospitable of islands they concluded that the islanders provided endless fascination for geneticists and anthropologists, as well as doctors. They found that the Pitcairn population were more disease-resistant (and, therefore, had a lower incidence of a whole range of diseases) than any society in the world. Even after two centuries of inbreeding they found a far lower incidence of genetic defects. To the investigating team, the record of mental health was most interesting; there were no psychoses, suicide was a thing unknown, and the feeders of criminality – alienation, major inequalities, jealousies, generation gaps – were entirely absent. Hence there was no crime. Ironic, this, when we consider the origin and early history of the Pitcairn Island race.

The 'immense strength' of both the men and the women on Pitcairn caught the attention of Ian Ball. The average height, he calculated, was 5 feet 10 inches, about the height of the tallest of the mutineers, Fletcher Christian. 'The one-big-family impression remained valid throughout the stay', said Ball.

Glynn Christian, the great-great-great-great-grandson of Fletcher through the Charles Christian line, chartered a schooner to follow the route to Pitcairn taken by his famous ancestor. He confirms the absence of crime and, therefore, forces of law and order on the island. 'There is an unbelievable spirit of generosity', he says. 'No door is ever locked; everyone is always in and out of everyone else's home. True enough, arguments do develop sometimes, but tomorrow they will be out in the longboats again. If two men cannot meet each other's eye they might drown. Hence differences are speedily resolved!'

Both Bali and Christian emphasized that Seventh-day Adventism is not as rigid as the popular legend has made it out to be. The Adventist concern with health and preventative medicine is very strong, but their 'recommended diet' is adapted to take account of the foods available on the island. It is highly probable that there is a connection between the Adventist diet and health principles, and the low incidence of disease on Pitcairn.

Ian Ball tells a story to illustrate the lack of legalism in the island's religious attitudes. He and his film crew arrived one day late because of stormy weather. Since it was the Sabbath and the sea was rough they did not expect the Pitcairners to come out the two miles from the shore to take them off their vessel. They had a pleasant surprise.

'Welcome to Peet-carn Island. We were expecting your sail yesterday.'

Ball apologized for arriving on the Sabbath.

'O-ah, did you think we'd let you sit out here in this? Church don't forbid it – coming out on Sabbath to help people.'

Commenting on Pitcairn's Sabbath, Glynn Christian says: 'The Sabbath is a tremendous day of joy and relaxation on Pitcairn. It is a family day. The Sabbath is the institution which keeps the community close-knit, and keeps the families intact. . . .'

Pitcairner Irma Christian, on a visit to England, though concerned to emphasize the strong religious tradition on the island, was also at pains to point out that the island was not problem-free. From time to time, she commented, there was evidence of resistance to Christianity on the part of some of the island's youth, and even a disinclination to attend church. She was concerned that too high a proportion of Pitcairn's youth were absorbed by the TV culture on New Zealand during the years of their secondary education and did not return to the island.

Ball was fascinated by the blend of cultures still evident on Pitcairn. He notes that the genetic balance favours the English, not the Polynesian. But he provides something for the geneticists to ponder: Pitcairn women are still a number of shade darker than Pitcairn men. On the mix of cultures:

'When the womenfolk wrap their foods in banana-tree leaves for the stone oven, or sit cross-legged on the ground weaving pandanus leaves, they present a picture of Polynesians garbed in the fancy dress of the white world. When the men talk engagingly of their "muskets", or put to sea in dirty weather, grim-faced in their hooded black oilskins, they are a remnant of a lost era of Englishmen, the descendants of sailors who wore pigtails and conquered the world. At services on the Sabbath the community strains to be impeccably *Anglo*. At a feast in the neighbours' home on Saturday night, once the sun has set on the Sabbath, they are unmistakably Polynesian in their gargantuan appetites and their uninhibited assault on the table's burden. In their passionate love of fishing, they remain close to their Tahitian ancestry. In their sentimental affection for the royal family they display an Englishness that has long since gone out of popular style in the home country.' – I. M. Ball, *Pitcairn: Children of the Bounty*, pages 212-213.

Photographs of the Queen, Prince Philip and the Prince and Princess of Wales were standard in almost every living room.

Glynn Christian is concerned, however, that the world shall understand that if Pitcairn is a paradise it is a fragile one. 'At present the economy of Pitcairn is so fragile that if, say, just *three* able-bodied men of the eight who man the longboats were drowned the island would have to be abandoned. The island needs regeneration.'

Pitcairn's total population is somewhere between fifty and sixty. Apart from the shortage of able-bodied men, what are the other factors which make the economy of Pitcairn so precarious?

'Pitcairn is more isolated than it was a century ago. Until twenty-five years ago freight and passenger vessels called by the island regularly, and the longboats would go out to meet them. There was a ship every two weeks, on average. Until very recently – because of the advent of the container ship and the popularity of jet travel – *only one ship a year* called in at the island. In the recent past the governor – who is also the British High Commissioner to New Zealand – has arranged for four ships a year to visit the island. But even this is not enough. . . .'

Are there no other links with the outside world? Glynn Christian continues: 'The phone link with New Zealand was installed only two or three years ago. Prior to that it was a case of Morse code and the telegraph system. The tenuous communication links with the outside world cause real problems. When a medical emergency arises the district nurse has to conduct the operation, receiving instructions from New Zealand by way of ham radio. Fear of medical emergencies is the most important single factor in causing people to move away from Pitcairn. Another factor is the need for education. Primary education facilities are available on the island, but beyond the primary level it is necessary for the children to go to New Zealand for their education. This entails a minimum of four years away from their home environment.' Like Irma Christian, Glynn Christian is concerned that too many are absorbed into a new way of life and do not return home.

1990 has been declared Pitcairn's bicentennial year. Glynn Christian is at the centre of plans to commemorate the anniversary. He confesses that he has an ulterior motive: 'We intend to use the bicentennial celebrations to draw the world's attention to Pitcairn's plight. . . .'

Regeneration is the key, apparently. But it 'does not mean everyone moving in and giving orders for immediate change', emphasizes Glynn Christian. 'Far from it. The idea to build an airstrip on the island, for example, has been abandoned since it would spoil the balance of the island and take up too much valuable agricultural land. However, it is desirable that a ship should call at the island at least once every four weeks. It is also desirable that sturdier types of building be adopted, that irrigation be introduced, and that existing crops be replaced with crops that are more pest-resistant.'

How is all this to be financed? 'Just off Pitcairn is Henderson Island, the last untouched, unexplored raised coral reef in the world. We propose to introduce a scientific establishment on it. Much of the finance would come from that.'

All accounts make it clear that Pitcairn is by no means a dying community. The island still has a cross-section of ages. The optimum population, however, is seen as about 150. Hence there is a clear need to attract back to the island Pitcairners who have moved away.

If the world has something to teach Pitcairn, is it possible that this tiny island community, surrounded by its vast *cordon sanitaire* of ocean has something to teach the world? Is it possible that Pitcairn, with its roots in breadfruits, buccaneers and Bibles, its short history contrasting the excesses of violence and promiscuity on the one hand, and with the benefits of the Christian new birth on the other, is the repository of values largely lost sight of in the West?

And is it possible that, insofar as we can balance the sophistications and technology of the West against the values prized by the land that time forgot, Pitcairn has the edge?

The names of William Bligh, Fletcher Christian, Matt Quintal, Edward Young, Bill McKoy, John Adams and the rest are still used by Pitcairners with a familiarity that might suggest intimate acquaintance. There is an immediacy about the island's history. Not a detail has been lost. The names of the headlands, bays, outcrops and forest clearings keep them alive.

The characters of that remote generation of hard-bitten,

pigtailed, seafaring men who took on the seven seas and met one morning in a never-to-be-forgotten confrontation on the decks of HMS *Bounty* are still very real in everyone's imagination. And when the strong men who ride the breakers in the longboats sing of 'a land that is fairer than day', and when the pastor in his pulpit preaches apocalypse, does there live in their imagination a tableau in which the entire cast of the story will be reassembled before a judge who is Redeemer and Father on the Last Great Day?

BIBLIOGRAPHY

PRIMARY SOURCES

William Bligh, *Log of the 'Bounty'.* Public Record Office, London.

William Bligh, *A Voyage to the South Sea, Undertaken by Command of His Majesty for the Purpose of Conveying the Bread-fruit Tree to the West Indies.* (1792). Institute of Historical Research, London.

Minutes of the proceedings of the Court Martial held at Portsmouth 12 August 1792 on Ten Persons charged with Mutiny on board His Majesty's Ship the 'Bounty'. (1794). Institute of Historical Research, London.

William Bligh, *An Answer to Certain Assertions Contained in The Appendix to a Pamphlet entitled: Minutes of the Proceedings on the Court Martial etc.* (1794). British Museum, London.

George Mackaness (ed), *A Book of the 'Bounty'.* A selection of primary source material relating to the *Bounty*'s voyage, the mutiny and its aftermath and sundry courts martial; including the correspondence of Bligh and the testimonies collected by Edward Christian. An introduction by Gavin Kennedy. (1981).

F. W. Beechey, *Narrative of a Voyage to the Pacific Performed on HMS 'Blossom'.* (1831). British Museum, London.

W. R. Dawson (ed), *Correspondence of Sir Joseph Banks.* (1958).

O. Rutter, *The Court Martial of the 'Bounty' Mutineers.* (1931).

SECONDARY SOURCES

Glynn Christian, *Fragile Paradise: the Discovery of Fletcher Christian, 'Bounty' Mutineer.* (1982).

Richard Hough, *Captain Bligh and Mr. Christian.* (1972).

Gavin Kennedy, *Bligh.* (1978).

H. M. S. Richards, *Mutineers on Pitcairn Island.* (1980).

David Silverman, *Pitcairn Island.* (1967).

H. L. Shapiro, *The Heritage of the 'Bounty': the Story of Pitcairn Through Six Generations.* (1936).

I. M. Ball, *Pitcairn: Children of the 'Bounty'.* (1974).

R. B. Nicholson, *The Pitcairners.* (1965).

Frank Clune, *Journey to Pitcairn.* (1967).

R. A. Young, *Mutiny of the 'Bounty' and Story of Pitcairn Island 1790-1894.* (1894).